SECOND EDITION

Marine Biology

An Introduction to Ocean Ecosystems

Amy Sauter Hill

Dedication

This book is dedicated to my parents,
Wesley and Marie Sauter,
for giving me my first glimpse of the ocean.

To my husband Ted for reminding me
to look inland every now and then.

To all my students, for teaching me
to have faith in the future.

And to my children, Katie and Emma,
the greatest gift of all.

1   2   3   4   5   6   7   8   9   10

ISBN 0-8251-4323-3

Copyright © 1995, 2002

J. Weston Walch, Publisher

P.O. Box 658 • Portland, Maine 04104-0658

www.walch.com

Printed in the United States of America

Contents

1. The Living Sea 1
2. Coral Reefs 9
3. Islands 23
4. Estuaries 31
5. Shallow Bays, Lagoons, and Inland Waterways 39
6. Subtidal Soft Bottoms 47
7. Sandy Beaches 53
8. Rocky Shores 61
9. Tide Pools 69
10. Kelp Forests 77
11. The Open Ocean 85
12. The Abyss 107
13. Polar Seas 113
14. Environmental Ethics: Approaching the Issues 127

Glossary 131
For Further Reading 135
Photo Credits 136
Index 137

CHAPTER 1 *The Living Sea*

I really don't know why it is that all of us are so committed to the sea, except I think it's because in addition to the fact that the sea changes, and the light changes, and ships change, it's because we all came from the sea.

JOHN F. KENNEDY

Earth is the water planet. Nowhere else in this galaxy or beyond has liquid water been found. This unique substance is essential to life on Earth. It is found in oceans so vast that light glistening from their surfaces can be seen in the far reaches of our solar system. What role have these oceans played in the drama of life? It was in these waters 3.5 billion years ago that life began. From that beginning, life developed and diversified to such an extent that the ocean seems like one huge organism. Growing, moving, changing, evolving, it truly is a living sea.

Ancient Oceans

Earth did not begin as a water planet. Four billion years ago it was hot and hostile, torn by violent volcanoes and earthquakes. Some scientists believe gases released from rocks during the eruptions formed huge clouds that eventually began to release rain. For many millions of years it rained on this planet, slowly filling the deep scars and basins left by Earth's violent beginnings. These first oceans blanketed the planet in water.

Rain dissolved salts from the rocks and carried them to the basins. The water eventually evaporated and rained down once again, but the salts always stayed behind and the ocean became salty. The salinity (salt content) of the ocean remains fairly constant today despite the continued deposition of salts. Sea spray blows water ashore to evaporate and leave behind its salty residues, while below the waves, in a far more gradual process, sedimentary beds form along the seafloor as salts and other minerals are drawn from the water.

The early oceans were filled with organic compounds in what has been called a "primordial [original] soup." Some energy source (the sun, lightning, or a comet) allowed these compounds, 3.5 billion years ago, to join together to form a primitive cell. This first cell is our most ancient ancestor and was the first life form on Earth. During reproduction, the cell's genetic material underwent countless changes that led to the formation of advanced cells, tissues, organs, and ultimately, whole organisms. This process of change is called evolution. It is possible to trace evolution through fossil evidence, embryonic development of organisms, and biochemistry, but no one can explain the moment when nonliving compounds came alive.

> 1. What is the link between humans and the sea?

The Process of Change

Today we know that the success of a species is determined by its ability to respond to demands made by its environment. Some will respond to these demands and will survive; others will not. Organisms that are fit will be able to reproduce, passing those traits to their offspring. Variations in the genetic material passed on from one generation to the next occasionally produce changes (mutations) in a species that make them even better suited to their environment. The members of the species that do not carry this new variation in their genetic material will be slowly replaced by the more fit population. This process is known as natural selection or "survival of the fittest."

> 2. Give an example of natural selection; choose any species.

The Importance of Habitat

An organism's environment plays the critical role in natural selection because it creates the circumstance that makes a given trait advantageous. This is true in a jungle, a desert, or an ocean. For this reason we will approach the study of marine life by examining the different environments within the ocean. Species that are particularly adaptable can be found in several habitats, while others have very specific needs and are only found in one. Only when we understand the nature of the habitat can we begin to appreciate the nature of the many creatures that live there.

> 3. Explain why it is necessary to study the habitat of an organism before we can understand its natural history and biology.

The ocean is composed of many unique habitats. The actions of currents, their temperature, the movement of waves and tides, the pressure exerted by water, and the topography of the ocean bottom all present important challenges to marine species.

Currents

Currents are steady flows of water that consistently move in a particular direction. Currents are generated by the movement of Earth on its axis, in a phenomenon known as the Coriolis force. Responding to this movement, huge circular rivers known as gyres are generated in the ocean. Currents are offshoots of these gyres. The topography of the ocean

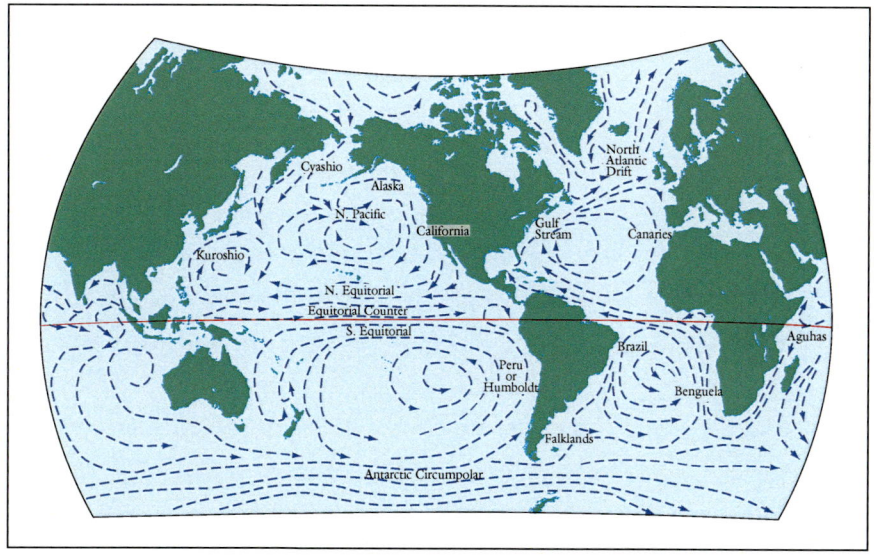

World ocean currents

THE LIVING SEA 3

bottom in combination with wind movement at the surface creates the flow of currents.

The Sargasso Sea is found hundreds of miles from shore, contained within a huge gyre in the Atlantic Ocean. Characterized by the floating seaweed known as sargassum, the boundaries of this sea shift with the surrounding currents.

> 4. Using the map of ocean currents, determine which current is responsible for the cold water off the coast of California. Explain your answer.

Temperature

The temperature of currents depends upon whether they are fed by polar or equatorial water. The Gulf Stream, fed by equatorial water, is a warm Atlantic current. The North Pacific, fed by polar water, is a cold Pacific current. Periodic shifts in prevailing winds can create changes in currents. Warm currents called **El Niño** (el NEEN yo) occur at these times, causing devastation to cold water species that cannot tolerate the temperature increase. Temperature also contributes to the way ocean water moves: cold water is dense and sinks, while warm water rises to the surface.

Temperature is not as great a consideration to marine organisms as it is to their terrestrial counterparts because temperatures do not change as quickly in the water as they do on land. There are exceptions to this, however, especially in the tide pools and other intertidal habitats (between the tides) where great fluctuations in temperature occur.

> 5. Why is water temperature more constant than air temperature?
>
> 6. What causes temperature fluctuations in intertidal habitats?

Waves

Most ocean waves are generated by wind moving over the water's surface. The highest part of a wave is called a crest, and the lowest part is called a trough. As waves move through the ocean, their crests become rounded and are able to travel for many thousands of kilometers, forming a swell. A wave breaks as it approaches shore because the shallow water it encounters creates drag, pushing the trough upward. A **tsunami** (su NAH mee) is a seismic wave or a wave generated by an earthquake offshore. Sometimes incorrectly referred to as tidal waves, tsunami are often huge and destructive. It is possible for tsunami to have crests 60 meters high.

Tides

Tides are the daily rise and fall of the ocean's water level caused by the gravitational pull of the moon and sun and the movement of Earth. More responsive than a solid, ocean water is pulled to one side of Earth by the moon's gravity. As the earth and moon revolve around each other, this bulge of water moves. Tides, then, are really just huge waves moving through the ocean in response to the position of Earth relative to the sun and moon. The wave's highest point is high tide and its lowest point is low tide.

On the east coast of the United States there are two approximately equal high tides each day. Parts of the Gulf of Mexico experience diurnal tides (one high and one low tide each day)—a rare tidal pattern. "Mixed" tides occur on the western coast of the United States, where each of the day's two high tides and each of the two daily low tides are of very different heights.

The Bay of Fundy, between Nova Scotia and New Brunswick, has the world's greatest tidal range (the difference between high and low tide). The tidal range of 15 meters in the bay is amazing when compared with the typical range of 1.5 to 3 meters along the coasts.

The low tide leaves this New England salt marsh exposed.

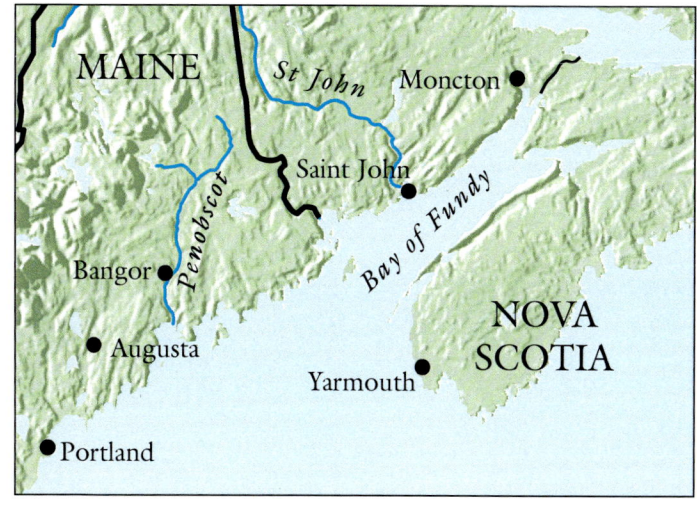

Bay of Fundy

> 7. Study the map of the Bay of Fundy and give a possible explanation for why the tidal range is so great.

Seasonal fluctuations in tide level occur because of the alignment of the sun and moon. Creating abnormally high and low tides, these cycles are important to the reproductive behavior of a number of animals in different habitats.

Pressure

At sea level, one atmosphere of pressure is placed on us at all times. Ascend a mountain and that pressure decreases, but enter the ocean and with each ten meters you descend the pressure placed on your body will increase by one atmosphere. Humans can only tolerate the pressure exerted up to about 100 meters beneath the surface. Marine organisms must also tolerate pressure. In the deepest ocean trenches they can be exposed to 1,000 atmospheres of pressure.

> 8. Why does water exert more pressure than air?

Those living things that are found in the dark ocean depths cannot survive at the surface, and those at the surface could not withstand the crushing pressures of the deep. Most animals live within a specific pressure range, moving up and down within certain boundaries. Some species are adapted to move between pressure extremes.

The Seafloor

The contours of the seafloor cannot be seen, but the oceanic landscape is rich and varied, with higher mountains and deeper trenches than elsewhere on Earth. The study of **plate tectonics** has shown that Earth is composed of a series of plates floating on a sea of fluid rock.

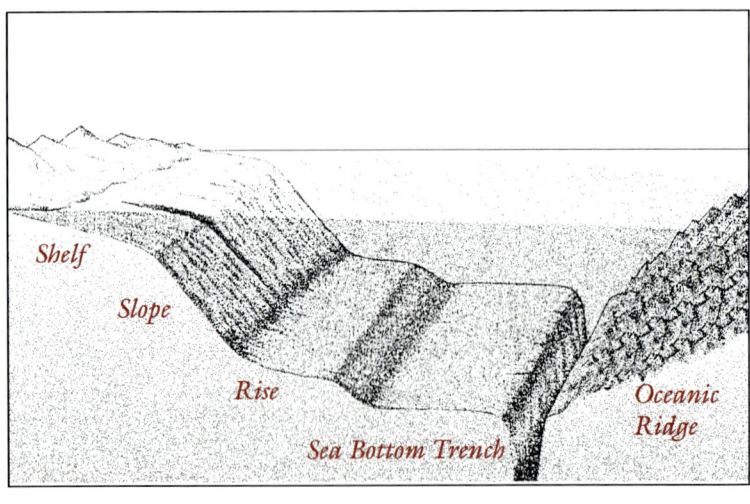

The ocean floor varies in depth from the shallow waters of the continental shelf to the deep ocean trenches—some as deep as 36,000 feet (about 11,000 meters).

On the Atlantic coast of the United States, the edge of the continent gradually slopes downward underwater along what is known as the **continental shelf.** At a point called the **continental slope,** this shelf drops sharply downward to the seafloor, leading to the deep ocean trenches. This slope is occasionally interrupted by a flattening feature known as the **continental rise.** Along our Pacific coast the change in depth is not as gradual. The seafloor drops sharply downward to the trenches much closer to shore.

The trenches are deep valleys in the seafloor. The deepest point in the ocean is the Marianas Trench (found in the Pacific Ocean), which extends 11,000 meters below sea level. These trenches lie along the borders of the huge plates.

It is not just the deepest features along the seafloor that are of interest to science. Earth's largest mountain range extends a total of 75,000 kilometers along the seafloor and is called the mid-ocean ridge. Submerged mountains are called **seamounts;** some have flat tops from erosive wave action and are called **guyots** (gee O).

Recent studies support the theory of seafloor spreading, according to which molten rock from Earth's mantle rises upward along the oceanic ridges, spread-

6 MARINE BIOLOGY

ing toward the continents. Once thought to be as old as Earth itself, the rock on the seafloor is relatively young; the youngest rock is found at the oceanic ridges. Since the new rock layers are not increasing the size of the seafloor and creating a more shallow sea, it is evident that some mechanism is at work to send rock back to Earth's mantle. Rocks push back down along the opposite borders of the huge plates in a process called subduction.

> 9. Compare the age of rocks on the seafloor with those on land. Which are older? Explain your answer.
>
> 10. Locate where you live on this map of Earth's tectonic plates. The plates move together and apart, over and under each other. Their boundaries are marked by mountain building and by earthquakes and volcanoes. What type of seismic activity is possible in your region? Which plates would be the cause?

Whether swimming through the swirling oceanic currents or clinging to a rock along the seafloor, the ocean's living things are of interest to marine biologists. What follows is a study of the organisms living within the many ecosystems of the sea.

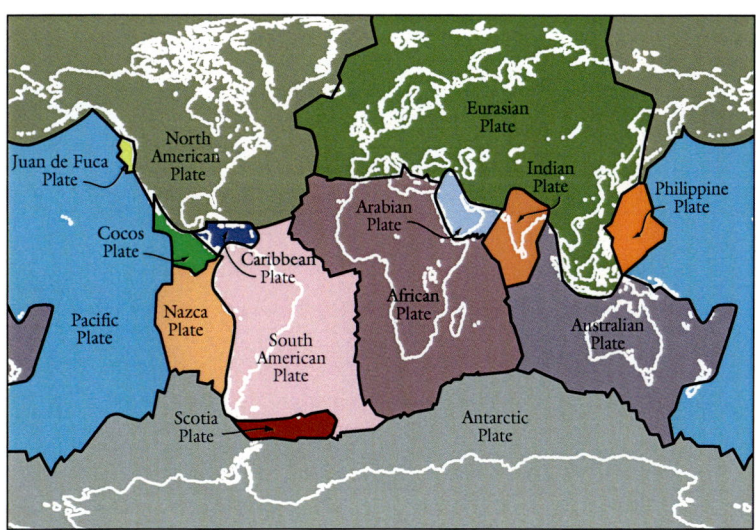

Tectonic plates

THE LIVING SEA   7

CHAPTER 2　*Coral Reefs*

Once our eyes and minds have digested the intricacy, the color, and the variety of this reef panorama, we feel touched by the essential tranquility. It is as if this scene were frozen in time. Unchanged, unchanging, the reef seems a haven of stability and peace in a world of tumult. Somehow, we instinctively feel it has always been thus. For eons before us and after us, the sea is the sea, and beauty dwells in the kingdom of coral.

CARL ROESSLER

The coral reef is home to the greatest variety of life in the ocean. Like huge underwater castles, these intricate structures are home to a fascinating network of life, with many examples of coexistence, cooperation, and competition.

Coral

Life in this ecosystem depends upon the corals. These tiny animals are classified as members of the phylum **Cnidaria** (ni DARE ee ah) because they have **nematocysts**—specialized cells used to sting and capture prey. Many species of coral growing together in one area form a reef. The corals may be either hard or soft depending upon whether they produce a stony skeleton to which other encrusting organisms can attach. Antler, brain, elkhorn, plate, saucer, and staghorn corals are all hard corals, while sea fans, sea pens, sea whips, organpipe coral, umbrella coral, sea pansies, and blue and red corals are all soft corals.

Corals exist as small **polyps** which secrete a skeleton to support themselves. The hard corals secrete a skeleton of calcium carbonate (limestone), called a **calyx** (KA lix), which remains after the polyp has died. Soft corals secrete a skeleton of **keratin** (a protein similar to that of fingernails), which will decompose. The calyxes of hard corals provide support to the living reef inhabitants that grow in, on, and around them.

Many inhabitants of the coral reef, like this queen angelfish, are strikingly colored.

Coral reefs can be one of three types: the fringing reef, the barrier reef, or the **atoll** (atolls will be discussed in Chapter 3, Islands). Fringing reefs grow in the shallows surrounding continents and islands. Barrier reefs serve as protective breakwaters to coastal areas. The Great Barrier Reef, the longest in the world, is 2,000 kilometers long and is located off the coast of Australia.

Corals come in many shapes and sizes, some forming colonies, others living alone. Their names reflect their great variety.

Algae and Sponges of the Reef

Hard corals do not build the huge limestone reef alone. **Coralline algae,** plant-like organisms that contain calcium carbonate in their cell walls for support, grow with the corals and help to strengthen the reef. In the aftermath of storms, when many coral colonies have been fractured, it is the coralline algae that quickly grow and bind the pieces back together.

10 MARINE BIOLOGY

Certain species of sponge also help to build the reef. Sponges are the simplest of animals because they lack tissues and organs; for many years they were classified as plants. Sponges consist of different types of cells coexisting within pore-filled support structures known as **spicules.** Sponges are members of the phylum **Porifera** (pore bearers). The spicules of different types of sponges are composed of different substances and are different shapes and sizes; some with hollow cavities provide an ideal habitat for other **invertebrates.**

The elkhorn coral, a hard coral, is named for its branching shape.

A large sponge may serve as home to hundreds of invertebrates, including brittle stars, shrimp, and worms. The sponge can function regardless of the presence of these guests, as its simple cells create a weak current from which food is gathered. A dead sponge continues to provide a home for these animals.

1. Why would sponges be classified as the simplest animals?

Zooxanthellae (zo zan THEL ee), single-celled green algae, live within the tissues of corals. In addition to assisting them in manufacturing calcium carbonate, they also provide food and oxygen through photosynthesis. The full extent of the corals' and the zooxanthellae's dependence on one another is not yet fully understood, but it is a fascinating aspect of coral reef studies.

The relationship between coral and zooxanthellae in part determines where coral reefs are able to grow. Reef-building corals can exist within the temperature range of 21 to 29 degrees Celsius (with the greatest variety occurring between 25 and 29 degrees Celsius). Corals also prefer shallow, calm waters, which light can easily penetrate, allowing the zooxanthellae to carry out photosynthesis. This

A coral reef supports a wide variety of life.

means that the vast majority of reef-building corals grow in tropical waters within latitudes 30 degrees north or south of the equator. Because tropical waters are low in dissolved oxygen, nutrients, and plankton, the abundant life found there is all the more impressive. These conditions make the coral reef a true oasis in the sea. The reefs are rich in invertebrates, countless species of which feed on the coral or the nutrients it generates. Nearly every phylum of invertebrate animal has a member living on the coral reef.

CORAL REEFS **11**

Predators of Coral

Corals face their share of invertebrate predators. **Nudibranchs** (NUDE i branks), shell-less members of the phylum **Mollusca,** class **Gastropoda,** feed on soft corals. Their name means "naked gills," and the feathery plumes on the dorsal side of the body are just that. These animals need shells only as embryos; their shells disappear as the animals mature. The soft-bodied adult nudibranchs are protected instead by offensive odors and mucous coverings that repel predators. One whiff or taste of a brightly-colored nudibranch is enough to drive away even a hungry fish or sea star.

After feeding on cnidarians, some nudibranchs even have the ability to keep the nematocysts (stinging cells) from their prey undischarged in their bodies for protection from predators. They swallow the nematocysts, store them in tiny sacs, and discharge them when needed from tubules at the body surface.

> 2. Why would bright coloration suit an animal whose main defense is bad taste?

A few other members of the phylum Mollusca—some cowries, flamingo-tongue snails, and sundial snails—also feed on soft corals.

The crown-of-thorns sea star is a coral predator, able to destroy large areas of living coral.

Bristleworms, members of the phylum **Annelida,** prey on the polyps of hard corals, attacking the vulnerable tips of the branching species. Bristleworms evert their mouths over the tips of the branching coral and release enzymes, digesting the polyp within its calyx and then absorbing it. Although it is an effective predator, the bristleworm does limited damage to the reef.

A member of the phylum Echinodermata (i KY ne der ma ta), the crown-of-thorns sea star also feeds on corals in this way, but can destroy large patches, up to 60 centimeters across in a single day. Since the 1960s, marine biologists have been concerned about the population explosion of these coral-eating sea stars and the irreversible damage they may do. Many plans for reducing their numbers were devised, but the sea star soon returned to normal numbers. Many hypotheses exist about the causes of the population increase, and most of them cite human activity. Natural predators of the sea star include giant clam, grouper, painted shrimp, pufferfish, triggerfish, and triton snail. Some feed on the sea star larvae, others on the adult animals. Human activities such as fishing and shell collecting may have led to a reduction in the numbers of these predators, allowing the sea star to overpopulate.

Weather conditions help to support another hypothesis. When it rains, freshwater runoff from land increases the amount of sediment and decreases the salinity on the reef. These conditions might allow more of the free-swimming sea star larvae to successfully settle and develop into adults.

Coral Reproduction

Corals reproduce either asexually by budding or sexually in a simultaneous release of egg and sperm into the surrounding waters. The tiny free-swimming zygotes will populate new areas, reducing competition for space.

Coral has many predators; it also has protectors. Certain species of shrimp and crab will attack the crown-of-thorns sea star to preserve their own homes. These tiny animals find both food and protection on living coral, so they are eager to protect their habitat. The shrimp and crab work together to drive the sea star away.

Fish on the Reef

Bony fish are a beautiful and essential part of life on the coral reef. Whether they feed on algae, coral, invertebrates, or other fish, all find food on the reef.

While many other fish throughout the ocean have **cryptic coloration** allowing them to hide, many of the coral reef fish advertise their presence. How this coloration evolved and why it persists is a mystery, but several possible explanations exist.

This four-eye butterfly fish is so named because of its brilliant coloration and rapid, butterflylike swimming motions.

The bright colors of the coral may serve to camouflage some fish from predator and prey. Others may use their bright colors to advertise their territories and their intent to defend them. Certain colors may identify members of a species. The more outrageous the color, according to this theory, the more likely the animal will be to find a suitable mate of the same species.

Although the dramatic colors and their combinations may make fish stand out for us, the same may not be true for their predators.

> 3. Explain what you see in the patterns of the four-eye butterfly fish that might protect it.

Some fish on the reef have no desire to hide or confuse predators. In much the same way as the nudibranchs advertise their bad taste, animals like the lionfish display their deadly battery of spines. These remind other fish that the lionfish can inflict a nasty, painful wound; the spines can contain deadly venom. The spines are found on long, modified fins that the lionfish also uses to herd its prey of small fish against the reef surface where they cannot escape.

The moray eel is seldom seen during the day. It emerges from its rocky den at night to hunt for fish along the reef.

Not all coral reef fish are brightly colored; as in so many other habitats, a good strategy for evading predators and deceiving prey is to hide. A type of scorpion fish (fish with deadly spines) called the rockfish is beautifully camouflaged in the rocks near the reef, but it is not hiding from predators. Instead, it is lying in wait for small fish, which it gulps into its huge mouth when they swim near. Rockfish are perhaps the best-camouflaged fish on the reef; divers often fail to see them from only a few centimeters away. Rockfish are also found in other habitats where rocks and other debris provide good hiding places.

Whether colored for hiding, advertising, or confusing, the bony fish all must gather food in some way and many feed directly on the coral. Parrotfish have beaks (fused teeth on the upper and lower jaw), which allow them to bite at the reef, and grinding structures in the digestive tract, which pulverize the coral. The parrotfish digests the polyps and algae within them, and the limestone, which is not digested, is voided as sand. Large expanses of coral sand lie just beyond the living reef as testament to the parrotfish's appetite.

The parrotfish can damage large areas of reef. However, studies show that when large herbivores like the parrotfish are prevented from feeding along an area of reef, the coral can be choked to death by the growth of algal mats that the normal grazing of the parrotfish keeps in check. It seems the "destructive" feeding of the parrotfish is a natural and necessary process.

> 4. How might such studies be conducted?

These same studies have found that some species of coral have chemicals that inhibit the growth of the algal mats. How the corals produce these chemicals is of great interest to biologists.

Some parrotfish feed delicately on the coral polyps, nipping at their calyxes with tiny mouths. Although the coral dies, this feeding technique opens areas for new growth and allows other invertebrates, such as fan worms, to make their homes in the empty limestone cups.

Fish have different body forms that allow them to exploit different areas of the reef. One particularly well-known reef dweller is the moray eel. Its long narrow body allows it to enter reef crevices, an important strategy in a habitat so filled with predators and prey. The sharp teeth of this bony fish allow it to inflict a bite, although it is usually shy. A nocturnal feeder, the moray eel hunts by smell. Only when disturbed in its den will the moray eel attack humans; one should never place a hand into a seemingly empty area of reef unless prepared for "sharp" consequences. Accounts of humans regularly feeding moray eels in the wild are true, although it is probably unwise to do so as the eels will lose their natural and justified fear of humans.

> 5. Why is it unwise to eliminate an animal's fear of humans?

Triggerfish are named for the **dorsal** spine that they erect for protection after entering reef crevices. Their large mouths allow them to feed on a number of different invertebrates, including the sea urchin. As the sea urchin moves over a sandy area on its tube feet, it is vulnerable, for the triggerfish can blow it over and reveal the soft mouthparts below. The urchin's spines are then useless. Triggerfish also bite protruding surfaces of coral and search through them for bivalves, **crustaceans,** or other animals that have burrowed into the coral.

The triggerfish has developed a technique for overcoming the sea urchin's defensive spines.

There is one fish on the reef that has an unusual body design for defense rather than for feeding. The porcupine fish, under normal circumstances, is a relatively small, placid animal that searches along the reef for crustaceans, echinoderms, and mollusks to eat. However, if it is frightened, it will rapidly draw water into its body and expand enormously in size. The spines, which lie flat before it inflates, are erected menacingly.

> 6. There are two ways in which this behavior can assist the porcupine fish. What are they?

To reproduce, several of the bony fish found on the coral reef have evolved nest-building behaviors. Many fish in the ocean are broadcasters—male and female release sperm and eggs simultaneously in the open water. Nest-building gives the egg and sperm a greater chance of encountering one another and the offspring a better chance of survival, but there is a price. Building and guarding a nest are energy-intensive activities.

Triggerfish make their nests in the sandy areas adjacent to the reef. The large dish-shaped excavations, sometimes 1.5 meters or more in diameter, are cleared when the triggerfish flaps its fins against the sand. It then makes a small cup in the center by blowing away sand with its mouth. The female lays her eggs in the center and the male fertilizes them. He then guards the eggs from predators and constantly patrols the borders of his territory.

Damselfish males prepare a nest of red algae on the reef on which the female can lay her eggs. The male fertilizes them and then chases the female away. He protects his young from hungry predators and uses his fins to create greater water movement, bringing them oxygen. The eggs and developing embryos are nutritious and delicious to other animals on the reef. The male damselfish will be kept constantly busy as he tries to keep predators at bay. Some young will inevitably be lost.

When frightened, the porcupine fish sucks in water to appear large and threatening.

7. What are the advantages of nest-building? What are the costs?

8. What must broadcasters do to reproduce that nest builders need not do?

Territories are not maintained just during times of breeding. Some species of angelfish fiercely defend their territories, chasing intruders and threatening them with a sharp spine on the **pectoral** fin. These tiny, colorful fish establish social rank within populations along a given stretch of reef. They are so sensitive to members of their own species in these communities, that if the dominant male is killed, the dominant female will become a male! The male's death triggers a hormonal change in the female that allows her to take over this important position in the population. Some species of wrasse also display this behavior.

9. Why would it be important to assure the availability of a dominant male?

10. How would you go about studying this behavior on the coral reef?

Symbiosis on the Reef

The coral reef is home to so many different kinds of life that interesting relationships for feeding and protection have developed. A partnership with members of another species that creates an advantage is called **symbiosis;** there are many symbiotic relationships on the coral reef.

16   MARINE BIOLOGY

Parasitism, commensalism, and **mutualism** are all forms of symbiosis. Parasitism harms one member and benefits the other; commensalism benefits one member and does not affect the other; and mutualism benefits both partners.

> 11. Name the examples of symbiosis that have already been mentioned in this chapter.

Cleaning symbiosis is a striking example of cooperation on the reef. Many fish are susceptible to external parasites that live between their scales and feed on their tissues. Whether the parasites cause discomfort is not known, but the fish do seek to remove the pests from their scales with the help of another animal. Butterfly fish, immature gray angelfish, gobies, peppermint cleaning shrimp, and cleaner wrasse all pick parasites off the bodies of other fish. Colored with a distinguishing bright blue and yellow band, the cleaner wrasse is the best-known cleaner. It chooses an area on the reef where local fish will come regularly to be cleaned—a cleaning station.

The cleaner wrasse has distinctive markngs to "advertise" its presence.

The cleaner wrasse swims over the entire body of its customer, picking parasites from the scales and even going into the mouth and gills of the fish to remove bits of food or other debris. If the fish has a wound, the cleaner wrasse will remove all damaged tissue, promoting healing. Fish at the stations open their gills to help the wrasse complete the cleaning. Fish that are normally aggressive seem to be on neutral ground as they wait to be cleaned; there is seldom any fighting at the station.

Since entering the mouth of a larger fish is not the safest of occupations, the cleaner wrasse sometimes vibrates its fins while cleaning between the teeth of its customers as a reminder of its presence. The wrasse is also given a form of immunity; it is not pursued by the larger fish because of its helpful ways.

Another fish that resembles the cleaner wrasse, the false cleaner blenny, takes advantage of the usually aggressive larger fish waiting to be cleaned. Mimicking a cleaner wrasse, it approaches the waiting fish, bites at the fins, and escapes with a mouthful of food.

> 12. What forms of symbiosis are evident in this cleaning phenomenon?
>
> 13. What does the cleaner wrasse receive from this arrangement?
>
> 14. Why does the cleaner wrasse need to be brightly colored?

Another form of symbiosis on the reef occurs between the banded goby and the pistol shrimp. The pistol shrimp has poor eyesight and is excellent at excavating holes in the sand surrounding corals. The banded goby has good eyesight but has no shelter from predators. These two animals have joined forces and now rely on one another for survival. While the pistol shrimp digs, the banded goby keeps watch for predators. If danger is near, the banded goby twitches its caudal fin to alert the pistol shrimp and both disappear into the hole. These unlikely "housemates" also stay together during the night, emerging safely from their shelter in the morning to begin another day of cooperation.

> 15. What form of symbiosis is this relationship?
>
> 16. What would be the fate of the banded goby and the pistol shrimp if they did not have each other?

The crinoid (KRY noyd), a member of the phylum Echinodermata, exhibits a form of symbiosis. A relative of the sea star, the crinoid has feathery plumes that filter **plankton** from the water. Numerous worms and shrimp remain on the plumes where they pick bits of food from the filtering apparatus. Some have highly-specialized coloration to remain camouflaged. The crinoid shows no ill effects from the relationship and seems to be unaware of its permanent house guests. The crinoid provides the perfect home for these small invertebrates.

> 17. What form of symbiosis is this relationship?
>
> 18. What form of symbiosis is this relationship in danger of becoming? Explain your answer.

Corals are not the only animals on the reef to benefit from the presence of algae. One of the most spectacular of all mollusks, the giant clam, keeps a population of zooxanthellae in its **mantle**—the tissue layer that secretes its shell. The giant clam, which can weigh one thousand kilograms, is wedged for life between the corals. The zooxanthellae, which flourish in the mantle, are given some protection while the giant clam, in addition to its filter feeding, feeds directly on the algae.

Simpler forms of symbiosis that help fish remain hidden also exist. The shrimpfish hides within the spines of the long-spined black urchin. The black stripe down its own body matches the spines of the urchin. Small prey can be caught from this safe vantage point. In a similar manner, the trumpetfish can hide inside a sponge and will suck small prey into its tubelike mouth as they pass by.

> 19. What form of symbiosis do these behaviors represent?

Cooperative relationships such as these, among so many different species, have caused biologists to call coral reefs the tropical rain forests of the sea. What these two ecosystems share is abundant life, astonishing variety of species, and prolific growth. Unfortunately, both rain forests and reefs are imperiled. Erosion, fertilizer in runoff, irresponsible fishing, damage from divers, overcollecting, and water pollution all threaten the world's coral reefs.

> 20. List several characteristics that coral reefs and tropical rain forests have in common.

Threats to the Reef

Living things that exist on the reef produce a certain amount of waste. Organic wastes include dead plants and animals, fecal matter, and **mucus.** Certain organisms eliminate this waste and prevent it from smothering the living reef. Crabs, shrimp, and lobster scavenge for dead organisms. Fecal matter, an important source of food, is consumed by worms, snails, and sea cucumbers. Bacteria decompose what is not eaten by other organisms.

Unfortunately, soil erosion from logging or agriculture has caused sediment runoff—more than can ever be processed by the working reef—to smother large areas. The island of Molokai in Hawaii is an example of an area where vast expanses of reef have been destroyed.

In Florida, steps have been taken to protect portions of the coral reef. Within the Florida Keys National Marine Sanctuary (established in 1972), "no-take" zones have been established where collecting coral is prohibited. Some 5,000 kilometers of coral-reef ecosystem are protected within the sanctuary. Boats are required to tie at moorings, permanent anchors placed near the reefs, rather than drop anchor.

Some fishing practices are a threat to coral reefs. One such practice, known as blast fishing, is deadly; it has cost many developing nations their living coral treasures. In blast fishing, fishers use dynamite and destroy vast expanses of the coral reef. A single bomb can destroy thousands of years of coral growth. The practice is prohibited but continues illegally.

Eager to bring the beauty of the sea into their own homes, people have provided a booming market for live fish for home aquariums. The bright colors of the coral reef fish make them among the most popular and the most expensive. Fishers, often from developing nations, use a technique to capture the fish that is devastating to the coral reef ecosystem. The fishers squirt large doses of bleach or cyanide—both highly poisonous—into the reef crevices to force fish hiding in them to flee. Stunned by the poison, the alarmed fish are easily captured. Many fish die immediately, while others die later from exposure to the poison. In addition, and perhaps most importantly, any living coral that is exposed to the cyanide or bleach will die.

> 21. What has to happen before this fishing practice will stop?

Cyanide and bleach are also used extensively to provide coral-reef fish for restaurants. Hong Kong alone imports 27,000 metric tons of live reef fish to be eaten each year. Among them are species of fish—for example, the humphead wrasse—which are considered to be depleted. Diners have been known to pay $175 to $300 for one plate of reef fish. The preference is for young fish that have not yet reached sexual maturity, fish that are captured and eaten before breeding. Despite bans on the export of the humphead wrasse, they are still imported in Hong Kong, where demand is high.

> 22. What are the dangers of capturing immature fish?

Corals have been harvested without regulation in many parts of the world for souvenirs, for use in aquariums, or for display pieces. In many areas, huge, healthy reefs have been all but destroyed by overcollecting. Black and red corals, widely collected for many years, are now extremely rare.

Scientists have recently discovered that a species of brown algae has been growing abundantly on the coral reefs of Florida and the Caribbean. This naturally occurring seaweed is smothering the coral. The cause of the unusually high growth is thought to be a combination of factors, including the disappearance of the black long-spined sea urchin, which feeds on seaweed. Its population was decimated by disease in 1983.

Extensive coastal development in the area has caused an increase in pollution, nutrient runoff, which is overstimulating the plant's growth. Reintroduction of the sea urchin should help; but tougher water-quality standards in Florida will be necessary to reverse the current trend.

> 23. How would a scientist determine whether the overgrowth of brown algae has been stimulated by pollution?

Global warming, the gradual increase in the earth's temperature due to greenhouse gases such as carbon dioxide and methane, is also having an effect on the coral reefs. It is not fully understood why, but when water temperature rises above a coral's normal range, the coral polyp expels its population of zooxanthellae. The cast-off algae dies while the coral polyp gathers in new algae. This coral bleaching often precedes the death of the coral and has increased dramatically in recent years. Although scientists agree that bleaching signals stress in these animals, some believe corals that bleach during sudden environmental change are more likely to survive. Bleaching may be an attempt to associate symbiotically with a species of algae better suited to the new conditions. Although it is not clear that bleaching is as devastating to coral as once thought, it is true that the human activities damaging to the reefs should be controlled. Ever-increasing temperatures and rising sea levels will demand the most of the coral's adaptive abilities.

Over the hundreds of millions of years that corals have been evolving in the sea, they have faced great changes, and the seas of today continue to provide similar challenges. Let us hope these coral kingdoms will continue to bring the color and exuberance of abundant life to the sea for a very long time.

CHAPTER 3 *Islands*

If once you've slept on an island
You'll never be quite the same
You may look as you looked the day before
And go by the same old name . . .
You may bustle about in street and shop
You may sit at home and sew
But you see blue water and wheeling gulls
Wherever your feet may go.
You may chat with the neighbors of this and that
And close to your fire keep
But you'll hear ship whistle and lighthouse bell
And tides beat through your sleep.
Oh, you won't know why, and you can't say how
Such a change upon you came
But once you've slept on an island
You'll never be quite the same.

RACHEL FIELD

Islands, isolated pockets of life, form along the coasts of continents and rise from the deep ocean. Some are pictures of paradise, but many more are remote and hostile to all but the most hardy of species. It is on and around islands that we can see firsthand the workings of natural selection; in their isolation, species evolve at a much faster rate than in more stable mainland ecosystems. Islands and the seas surrounding them have been throughout history the site of dramatic geological and biological dramas.

> 1. Why would species evolve faster on an island than they do in a mainland ecosystem?

Island Formation

Islands are among the most active of Earth's rocky features, as many were formed by volcanic activity. They provide geologists with a glimpse of the workings of Earth's interior. Hawaii is an example of a volcanic island chain. These islands, considered the most remote land masses on Earth, are found deep in the Pacific, 4,000 kilometers from the nearest continent.

The Hawaiian Islands exist because of the presence of a hot spot, an area on the ocean floor from which lava spews. Over many years, the liquid rock pours forth into chilly seas where it is quickly cooled, building up slowly until it breaks the surface of the water and becomes an island. Each of the islands of Hawaii was formed this way. Geologically speaking, these islands are infants, their rocks telling us they were created between five million and seven million years ago. In their shallows, corals colonize forming reefs.

> 2. In view of Hawaii's hot, hostile beginnings, what is most noteworthy about these islands today?

Not all of the islands of Hawaii have active volcanoes. The hot spot that created the islands remains stationary, but the islands themselves move ten centimeters north each year on the massive tectonic plate on which they exist. As they move further away from the hotspot, the older islands lose their source of lava and no longer grow in size. New islands form over the hot spot and the old slowly erode away.

The volcanoes, active or not, can be enormous. Mauna Kea rises 9,000 meters from its base on the ocean floor to its summit. Measured in this way, it is the most massive mountain on Earth.

Smaller islands in Hawaii were formed when a volcano no longer erupted and eroded away. Still surrounded by coral reefs, the sunken cone fell below the waves, creating a lagoon surrounded by the reef. Land built up on the coral reef, creating a small island known as an atoll. Atolls are very susceptible to storms, as they can easily be flooded.

Laysan Island, a small atoll in Hawaii, is the breeding site of a number of interesting seabirds: the ferry tern, the Layson teal, the Layson albatross, the red-tailed tropicbird, and the sooty tern. Endemic to Hawaii are 6,000 species found nowhere else on Earth.

Coral reefs contribute to the formation of other types of islands as well. The coral sand and rock generated by the living reef can build up in an area, creating land above the water. Such an island is called a key. The Florida Keys formed in this way. Coral rock, formed when coral sand and rubble are pressed together under pressure, helps to stabilize the islands as do mangroves, salt-tolerant trees that take root in the sediment. Birds such as brown boobies, crested terns, and pelicans are drawn to the isolated islands to nest and feed in nearby waters.

> 3. How are keys and atolls alike? How are they different?

The Galápagos Islands

The Galápagos Islands, about 1,000 kilometers west of Ecuador in the Pacific Ocean, are volcanic in origin but have very few corals. The waters surrounding these islands, despite their position on the equator, are fed by the cold Peru Current that brings nutrient-rich water from the deep ocean. The varied marine organisms that live in these waters rely on the current for survival.

Schools of fish fill the waters as do their many predators; it is not uncommon to see ten-foot hammerhead sharks cruising by. Green turtles are endangered everywhere else in the world, but here they live in abundance. The most northerly species of penguin is found on these islands; others live in the Antarctic, South Africa, Australia, and along the southerly coasts of South America. Blue-footed boobies and their relatives nest here along with flightless cormorants, which are unable to fly but can dive into the sea for fish. Dolphins and other whales—even the rare sperm whale—swim peacefully here as do the Galápagos sea lions, a subspecies of the California sea lion. The ocean's only lizard, the marine iguana, also finds a home in the Galápagos Islands. Having survived great journeys to arrive here, all have found success in this isolated world.

> 4. How might the marine iguana have arrived on the Galápagos Islands?

Best known for their influence on Charles Darwin's ideas on evolution, the Galápagos Islands are living monuments to the tenacity of those species that were able to adapt and survive on them.

In a world free from terrestrial predators, Galápagos Island species never developed a fear of humans, making them easy to approach. For many species, this is a great disadvantage, as they were hunted to near extinction by passing vessels. Even the expedition of HMS *Beagle,* in which Charles Darwin took part, held dozens of Galápagos tortoises on board for use as food. The strength of the long-living beasts was an advantage to these seamen; a tortoise would remain alive for many weeks without food and served as a source of fresh meat. The islands served as a stopover for ships; the crews decimated the tortoise populations. Lonesome George, the only known survivor of the Pinta Island tortoise, is a reminder of how quickly we can hurt populations of island species. The last female of this species was killed by fishers in 1980.

Santa Cruz Island, a continental island, was once part of the California mainland.

Other Galápagos species have been threatened through the years as well; the greatest perils today come from overfishing and the tourist trade. In a rush to provide sea cucumbers for consumer markets, fishers took 10 percent to 15 percent over the legal limit of slow-growing Galápagos sea cucumbers in 1994. The population is very slow to rebound, and concern for the health of the species continues. Fish populations everywhere face great pressure from overfishing; fragile areas such as the Galápagos Islands seem particularly vulnerable.

The great number of visitors every year to the Galápagos Islands places stress on an already fragile ecosystem. However, both the Ecuadoran government and conservation groups worldwide are committed to island preservation. Impact from visitors is closely monitored. In January 2001, an oil spill in the water surrounding the islands underscored how important it is to protect these unique places. The oil damaged some coastline but has been contained.

> 5. What can we learn from the fate of the Galápagos tortoise?

Continental Islands

Still other islands form when land breaks away from a continent and slowly moves away from it due to tectonic plate movement. The distance between the island and continent increases over time and they become isolated from one another. The Channel Islands are continental islands just west of Southern California.

The coastal islands of Maine are also continental islands, but they were greatly altered by the last ice age when they were completely covered by the polar ice cap. As it melted, the land rebounded, creating a shoreline much more varied than it was before the ice descended.

> 6. Why would ice make a difference in the topography of the shoreline?

Caribbean Islands

Found in the warm equatorial waters of the Atlantic Ocean, the islands of the Caribbean are geologically quite active. Some islands in this chain experience earthquakes from the movement of the Caribbean Plate on which they ride. (See plate tectonics, p. 6.) Others are volcanic in origin and have active volcanoes. Still others have formed by the upward push of sediments along plate boundaries. The Bahamas have formed a shallow sea from the stretching and weakening of the section of Earth's crust on which they lie. The Caribbean islands are a platform of oolite, mineral grains of evaporated calcium carbonate on the seabed. The island of Bermuda, east of North Carolina, rests on an extinct volcano capped by coral rock. The Caribbean islands, affected by the Gulf Stream, are sometimes called "islands in the stream." Their waters are warm, within the narrow range of temperatures most corals find livable, so corals colonize the islands' fringes.

The tiny island of Bonaire in the Caribbean provides us with an excellent example of the benefits of protecting natural spaces. To stop coral-reef destruction, the seas surrounding the island were declared a marine park in the 1970s. The island now boasts a flourishing tourist economy. Visitors are instructed how to behave underwater to minimize their impact on the ecosystem.

> 7. What can we learn from the commitment to nature made by the people of Bonaire?

New Zealand

New Zealand lies on the active faults between the Pacific Plate and the Australian Plate, making it one of the most seismically-active areas in the world. This geologic activity has led to the formation of the mountain ranges and the lowland basins for which New Zealand is well-known. The submerging crust of the Pacific Plate creates volcanoes throughout the country. On the other side of the ocean this same movement of the Pacific Plate has split Baja from the continent, creating the Gulf of California. New Zealand has a marine reserve system that protects 4 percent of its territorial waters; the hope is to expand to 10 percent. The reserves represent a huge diversity of ecosystems.

Barrier Islands

Other islands along continents are formed by the action of sand and dunes. On the east and gulf coasts of the United States, where the continental shelf is large, wave action readily forms sand. This sand can build up as a large bar offshore, which eventually rises above the waves. Grasses take root in the shifting sand and help to stabilize it. Such areas are called barrier islands since they create a wave barrier for the shore. Despite the presence of grasses, barrier islands move significantly over time.

During the last ice age, the level of the sea was 90 meters below what it is today. Water was frozen in the polar ice caps, which then were much larger. The continental shelf was exposed to violent wind and wave action, creating sand. As the ice age passed, the polar ice melted and the sea level began to rise, forming sandbars and islands. As the sea level continued to rise, the barrier islands moved toward the shore and some even joined the coast, while new sandbars and islands formed offshore. About 3,000 years ago, the rise in sea level slowed and the barrier islands stabilized, but they continue to move toward land. The nature of sand will always cause barrier islands, like the Outer Banks of North Carolina, to shift.

Dunes on Pea Island, North Carolina, a barrier island, part of the Cape Hatteras National Seashore.

> 8. Why would a large continental shelf be necessary for the formation of barrier islands?

Threats to Island Ecosystems

In an effort to hold back the sea, humans build breakwalls, **groins, jetties,** and **seawalls**—called hard stabilization. The practice is controversial because it can damage beaches and barrier islands. Structures extending from the shore are designed to reduce wave action so that sand will not be carried away and beaches will not erode. Studies have shown, however, that preventing one beach from eroding starves another. If the natural movement of the sand is interrupted, beaches will erode. Barrier islands naturally shrink and grow. Homes are built too close to the beach, and measures are taken to maintain the properties. Such building practices have led developers to ask for hard stabilization to prevent erosion, yet other beaches on the islands suffer as a result.

Although islands are frequently far from continents, they are never far from human influence. In many cases, the negative consequences of human activity are magnified on islands.

Hawaii is home to many plants and animals found nowhere else on Earth. Continued pressure from development has placed several species in danger of extinction. As more and more golf courses, hotels, and homes are built in Hawaii, more and more endemic species will disappear. Land management in Hawaii has been a bumpy road. For example, on these islands, where the only indigenous animal is the bat, rats were brought by the first European ships on Captain Cook's expeditions. Free from natural predators, the rats quickly overpopulated. They placed great pressure on shy endemic birds which were unaccustomed to such predators. Feeding on birds' eggs and young, the rats quickly endangered many species. Much later, mongeese were brought to the island to kill the rats, but no one remembered that rats are nocturnal and mongeese are diurnal. Not only did the mongeese not encounter the rats they were brought to eliminate, they also began to threaten the ground-dwelling birds by feeding on their eggs.

Agricultural demands have imperiled native plant populations on many islands. Sugar cane and pineapple groves have replaced many native forests in Hawaii. Goats are also a problem on Hawaii. Escapees from domestic stock, they now roam freely, overgrazing all native vegetation. Pigs on the Galápagos Islands are threatening green sea turtle populations because they dig up and eat turtle eggs laid on the beaches. On the Island of Catalina, owned in part by the Catalina Island Conservancy, goat populations have been controlled and native plant populations have rebounded.

> 9. Why is it of particular significance to island species when such introductions take place?

Secluded islands beckon the spirit of adventure in us all. Yet even as we dream of the rugged splendor, solitude, and protection they provide, let us not forget that it is we who must do the protecting.

> 10. How is planet Earth like an island? Explain your answer.

CHAPTER 4 *Estuaries*

Estuaries are a happy land, rich in the nutrients of the continent, stirred by the forces of nature like the soup of a French chef, the home of myriad forms of life, from bacteria to protozoans to grasses and mammals; the nursery, resting place, and refuge to countless species.

STANLEY A. CAIN

Where freshwater flows from the land and mixes with salt water from the ocean in protected coastal areas, an **estuary** (ES choo air ee) forms. Estuaries are also referred to as coastal wetlands and all contain some brackish water (a mixture of salt and fresh). Exposed to the daily rhythms of the tides, in combination with freshwater runoff, organisms that live in the estuary must tolerate huge fluctuations in salinity. Estuaries are also characterized by different substrates. Sand and mud are deposited in varying depths and provide homes to a number of plants and animals. The largest estuary in the United States is the Chesapeake Bay, which drains the watershed from six states.

Plants of the Estuary

Both salinity and **substrata** are key factors for the estuaries' most important life form—vascular plants. Salt quickly kills most plants, but remarkably the vascular plants found in the estuary are able to remove excess salt from their tissues by means of special pores. Taking root in the sand or mud of the estuary, they create living space and provide nutrients for the myriad animals that exist there. A key factor in their ability to take root is the absence of direct wave action on the sheltered coasts where estuaries are found.

Mudflats like this one in Massachusetts provide both food and shelter to a variety of animals.

As in most ecosystems, photosynthetic plants and protists are the primary producers. Harnessing the sun's radiant energy and forming food is just the beginning. Decaying plant parts, those which are shed as the plant grows, are an essential source of food for animals in the estuary. A few feed directly on the newly-shed material while others must wait for it to be partially decomposed. Bacteria and fungi (decomposers) consume the dead plant parts, releasing inorganic materials called **detritus** (de TRY tus), which are used again by the plants. This important nutrient is also carried offshore with the tide and is important to other marine habitats.

1. What causes variation in salinity in an estuary?

2. Why are decomposers important in a food chain?

3. Why is detritus such an important nutrient in estuaries?

In temperate waters, Spartina grasses characterize estuaries known as salt marshes. Cordgrass can be found in the lower marsh, and salt marsh hay in the high marsh. In tropical and subtropical waters, estuaries composed of mangroves, which must have warm temperatures to survive, are called mangrove swamps. In areas closest to the ocean, where marsh grasses and mangroves cannot tolerate being completely submerged, sea grass communities are able to colonize. Turtle and eel grass are examples of sea grasses in these areas. Areas where no plants grow at all are called mud flats. All of these estuarine communities support their own array of interesting plant and animal life.

> 4. Name and describe the four estuarine communities.
>
> 5. What are the key factors in determining where an estuarine plant or animal will grow?
>
> 6. Why are Spartina grasses and mangroves not found in the same area?

Invertebrates in the Estuary

The estuaries are home to many interesting invertebrates. The roots of cordgrass in the low marsh provide both food and attachment sites for barnacles, mussels, and periwinkles. The barnacles and mussels attach themselves permanently and filter detritus from the surrounding water. The periwinkles graze on algae as they move up and down the stem of the grass.

In the high marsh, fiddler crabs feed on detritus at low tide and retreat into their burrows at high tide; their claw-waving territorial and mating displays are highly visible. Marsh snails also feed on detritus at low tide, but seek shelter from high tide by climbing up the stem of salt marsh hay, which is never fully submerged. These tiny snails extract oxygen from the atmosphere, not the water.

The tiny periwinkle can be seen throughout the estuary, grazing on algae.

The sprawling roots of the mangroves are small, shadowy worlds filled with life. The large roots provide attachment sites for anemones, hydroids, sea squirts, and sponges, while the swimming space between the roots provides shelter for shrimp, crabs, and small fish.

The mudflats provide a home to a different set of invertebrates. Nutrients carried to the mudflats from other parts of the estuary settle on this soft substrate and are exploited by a number of different burrowers. Clams, crabs, worms, and a vast array of microscopic organisms—protists, round worms (phylum Nematoda) and copepods (phylum **Arthropoda**)—all live in or on the muddy sediment. Since little oxygen can penetrate beyond the first few inches of sediment, these animals remain near the surface. Feeding on detritus, these animals are important in cycling nutrients back into the food chain, as they are preyed upon by fish, shrimp, and larger animals.

Bivalves, members of the phylum Mollusca, are ideally suited for life in the estuary; members of this class include clams, mussels, oysters, and scallops—all filter feeders. They are protected from most predators and from the crushing weight of the sediment in which they burrow by the two hinged shells for which they are classified. Clams generally burrow into mudflats, filtering food from the water above with a muscular siphon. The depth to which they burrow depends upon the length of their siphon.

Oyster beds first form when larvae settle on a shell or other bit of debris on the top of a mud flat. As these oysters become established, their young attach to them and a large colony can grow. Barnacles, hydroids, seaweeds, sponges, and tube worms also are able to attach to the oysters and an entire community is formed.

Oysters also offer a base for parasites. Eggs of the oyster drill—one of the worst parasites on oysters—are attached to the oyster in the center of this picture.

In the sea grass communities, scallops develop; in fact, without the sea grass for attachment the scallop larvae would die in the soft sediment. Scallops are fascinating animals and although seemingly sedentary are quite mobile. When startled in the sediment where they filter food, adult scallops are able to shoot a stream of water out of their shell and burst into movement. They cannot move over large distances in this way, but they are able to avoid slow-moving predators such as the sea star. Adult scallops also have as many as 50 blue eyes found in the fleshy muscle between the two shells.

7. Why are bivalves well adapted to life in the estuary?

Seasonal Species of the Estuary

The large populations of invertebrates, nutrient-rich and calm waters, and abundant shelter all bring many seasonal or migratory species to the estuary. Many fish, including striped bass, bluefish, menhaden (men HAY den), and surfperch are found in estuaries as juveniles. They will use the available food and shelter to gain size and strength for the competitive adult lives they face in the open sea.

The presence of these young fish among other food sources makes the estuary a haven for both seasonal and year-round populations of birds. Birders travel great distances to the estuaries to view the many species found there.

Estuary Birds

All birds (class Aves) have feathers. These durable, lightweight structures not only insulate, but also help to direct air over the wings to create lift. While all birds also have forelimbs modified as wings, not all are able to fly. The design of a bird's body—beak, feet, legs, and wings—will determine what food it will be able to gather. Varying body designs allow the animals to exploit different food sources and habitats.

The herons, with their long legs and sharp beaks, stalk and then spear small fish. Several species, including the regal great blue heron, can be found in the estuary all summer long.

Sandpipers include curlews, dowitchers, godwits, plovers, ruddy turnstones, sanderlings, sandpipers, and willets; all have probing beaks of varying lengths. They are capable of searching for small invertebrates in the mud. They also search for food on sandy beaches, dodging out of the way of breakers within the surf zone.

Pelicans, both brown and white, can be found feeding in estuaries, although their feeding techniques are different. The white pelican scoops up prey while swimming along the surface. Brown pelicans hurl themselves from the air into the water to scoop prey with their enormous beaks. Although they seem ungainly, they are streamlined and efficient during their dives. Nearly extinct after the use of DDT weakened their eggshells, these birds can now be found either in the estuaries or along sandy beaches, often gliding peacefully along the waves. When flying in groups, the brown pelicans will "follow the leader," beating their wings or gliding only when the lead bird does so.

> 8. What might be the advantage of flying in this manner?

The black skimmer is a rare and beautiful bird that regularly visits the estuary. This relative of the tern is the only bird whose lower mandible is longer than the upper. With the lower mandible in the water, these birds glide close to the surface in order to capture small swimming prey.

Osprey are the only exclusively fish-eating birds of prey and their shrill, distinctive call is one of the beautiful sounds of the estuary. Like so many other birds, they were devastated by the use of DDT, but have made a remarkable comeback.

Many species of duck and goose may also winter in the estuaries, usually preferring those areas that are predominantly freshwater. Ideally suited to float and feed, these birds gather aquatic vegetation with their shoveling beaks.

> 9. Does this mean different species of birds do not compete with one another? Explain.

Manatees and dugongs, members of the order Sirenia, sometimes wander into estuaries to feed and rest. These quiet mammals are tolerant of the salinity changes that take place in estuaries and seem well suited for the warm, calm waters there.

Threats to Estuary Ecosystems

Like the other animals drawn to these unique areas, humans also come to the coast, but their effect is not always a positive one. Estuaries are being destroyed at an alarming rate to make room for marinas, homes, and other coastal developments. On the Pacific coast of the United States, 91 percent of the coastal wetlands have been lost. The remaining 9 percent face ecological isolation because they are surrounded by human habitation. The National Estuarine Research Reserve System protects 425,000 acres in 18 states and Puerto Rico, but other estuaries must be protected as well.

Dredging, the periodic removal of bottom sediments to maintain water depth for ship navigation, disturbs bottom-dwelling organisms and increases the suspension of sediments in the estuary. The sediments dredged up must be disposed of, which causes another problem: inhabitants of areas on which the sediments are dumped will be smothered and die.

The brown pelican is now a common sight along the coasts of the United States.

The very nature of estuaries as the meeting place of fresh- and salt water places them in great danger from toxic runoff. Pesticides, in many areas only marginally regulated, are harming many estuaries as they flow to the sea through rivers and streams. Concentrated, especially after rain, these pollutants taint shellfish and kill other wildlife like birds and fish. Many once-rich shellfish areas have been closed to fishing as contaminants make the animals unfit for human consumption.

It is important to recall that the nutrients from the estuary move offshore with the tides and nourish living things in other habitats.

Salt marsh of Upper Newport Bay, California.

10. Look at the picture of Upper Newport Bay, California. Which of the pressures on this ecosystem are evident in the photo?

ESTUARIES 37

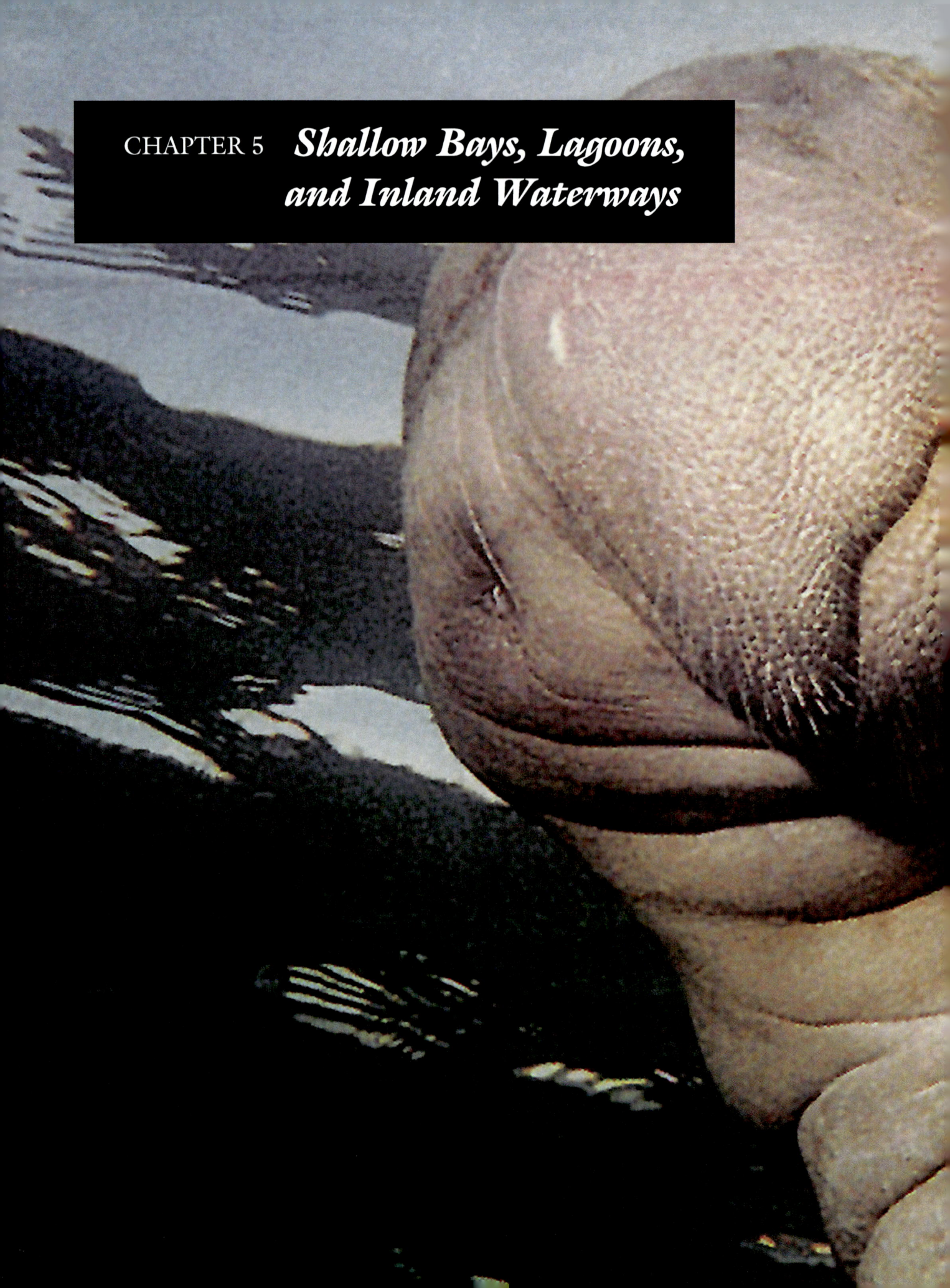

CHAPTER 5 *Shallow Bays, Lagoons, and Inland Waterways*

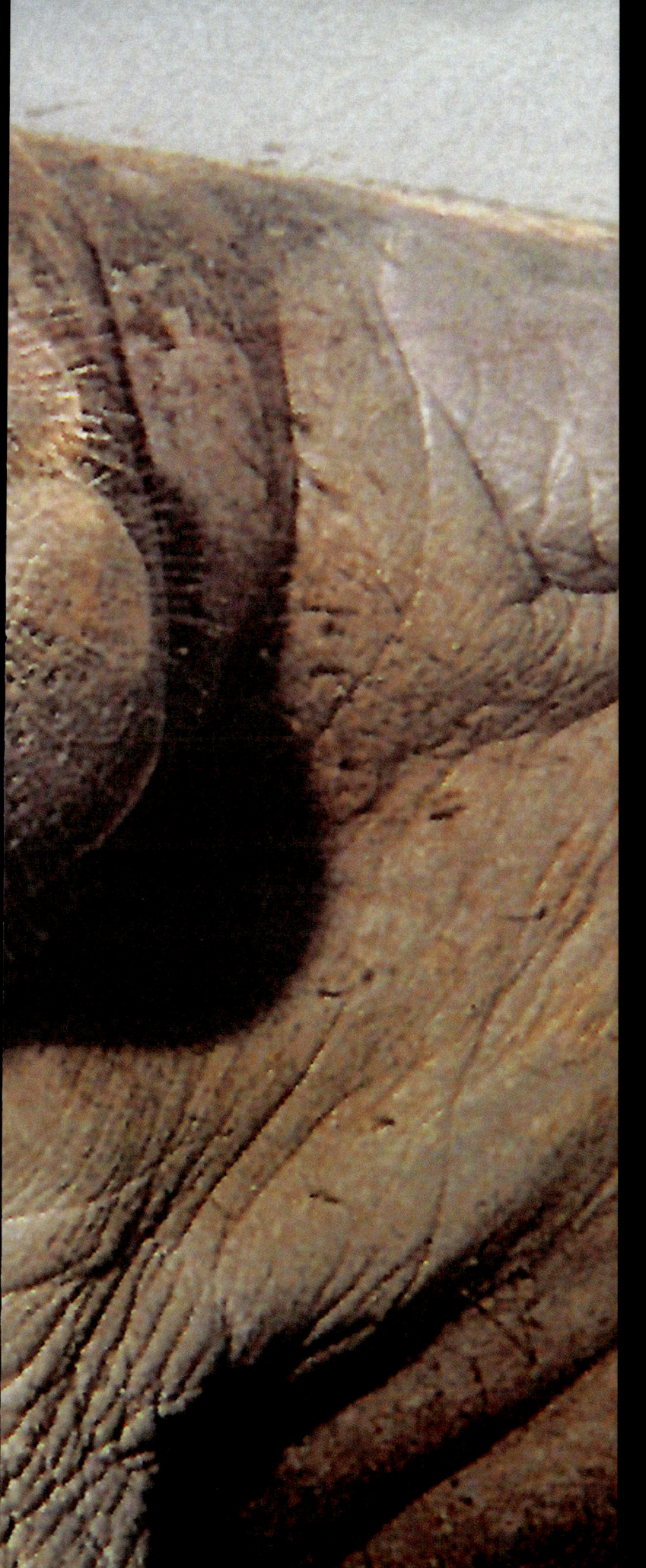

Everyone must be struck with astonishment when he first beholds one of these vast rings of coral-rock often many leagues in diameter, here and there surmounted by a low verdant island with dazzling white shores, bathed on the outside by the foaming breakers of the ocean and on the inside surrounding a calm expanse of water, which, from refelection, is of a bright but pale green color.

CHARLES DARWIN

Not all coastlines are exposed to pounding surf. Protected lagoons and bays provide food and shelter to a few animals and plants. Lagoons are sometimes formed as a coral reef island evolves, while others exist along sheltered coasts. Inland waterways that are affected by the tides also serve as important habitats.

These bays, lagoons, and inland waterways are inextricably bound to life within other habitats including coral reefs, sandy beaches, and estuaries. Many plants and animals found in these calm bays can also be found in other habitats.

Although these sheltered habitats vary greatly, sea grasses are able to take root in almost all of them. Like the sea grass communities that develop in estuaries, these plants bring some stability as their roots cling to shifting sand. Dependent invertebrates such as snails and scallops find homes here, as do small fish.

1. Why might shallow bays be found near coral reefs, sandy beaches, or estuaries?

Horseshoe Crabs

One particularly interesting animal is the horseshoe crab—a member of the phylum Arthropoda. In the spring, horseshoe crabs come into the estuaries and shallow bays to take advantage of the seasonal high tides. They deposit their eggs above the highest tide, as salt water will kill their embryos if they are exposed to it too early in development.

The smaller males cling to the females throughout the long journey from the open sea. Carried on the waves of the high tide, the female with the attached male crawls up into the high marsh to dig a shallow nest. The male fertilizes the eggs as the female deposits them into the nest. Since the tide has receded by the time this process is finished, the two must temporarily burrow into the soft sand to await the next high tide that will then carry them back to open water. In two weeks' time, when the spring tides are again as high, the force of the waves on the developing young will burst their egg cases and they will be released. The young crabs will feed on detritus before they enter the open water where they will live out their adult lives. Fossil evidence indicates that the horseshoe crab has remained unchanged for 200 million years.

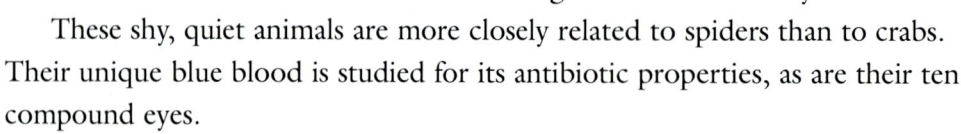

These shy, quiet animals are more closely related to spiders than to crabs. Their unique blue blood is studied for its antibiotic properties, as are their ten compound eyes.

No pressure on the horseshoe crab over the last 200 million years has prepared it for the devastation of eel fishing. Eel fishers trawl or collect horseshoe

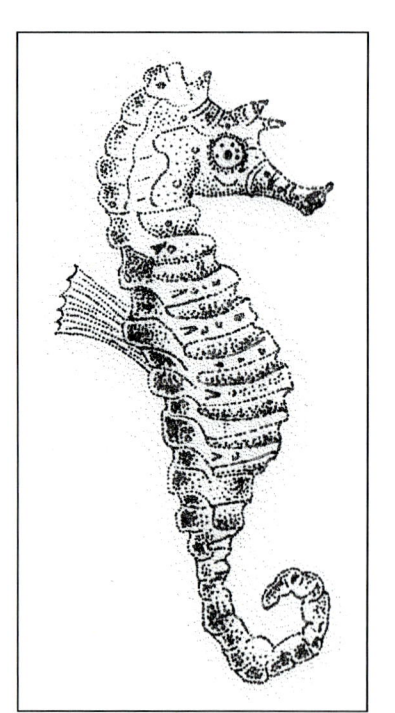

The sea horse swims in an upright position, propelled by a dorsal fin that beats about 35 times a second.

crabs for bait from the beaches where they leave the water to mate and lay eggs. Tens of thousands can be captured by **trawling** in a single day.

Population studies since 1990 show a 50 percent drop in horseshoe crab numbers. In some states agreement has been reached with eel fishers to enforce quotas to reduce the impact on horseshoe crabs; only a certain number can be collected in a given time.

Fish

One species of bony fish seems to be ideally suited for life in the grass of shallow bays. The pipefish, named for its long, thin body, so closely resembles a blade of grass that it is almost impossible to see. It even waves back and forth with the slight swell so that its movements fit perfectly with its surroundings.

A relative of the pipefish, the sea horse (placed with the pipefish in the family Syngnathidae), is found in several other habitats in addition to protected bays. Its tail allows it to grasp grass and rocks for attachment while it waits to suck zooplankton into its tubelike mouth. Male sea horses protect their developing young inside a pouch. Females lay their eggs inside the pouch where the male fertilizes them. The young remain inside the pouch for protection until ready to emerge. The male then twists and turns to expel the young from the pouch as if giving birth.

Sea horse populations are declining rapidly due to the destruction of their coral reef, estuary, mangrove, and shallow-bay habitats. Some are caught for the aquarium trade, but 95 percent of captured sea horses are sold for use in traditional Asian medicines. Twenty million animals are sold each year, primarily in Hong Kong, as treatment for various common ailments.

Two relatives of the sea horse, the leafy and weedy sea dragons, are highly specialized fish that conceal themselves in the floating vegetation in the near-shore waters of parts of Australia. Perfectly camouflaged with modified fins, they float effortlessly in the shallows. Many are captured for the aqarium trade, but the animals are hard to keep and few survive. Measures have been taken in Australia to protect them, but illegal fishing continues to pressure the depleted population.

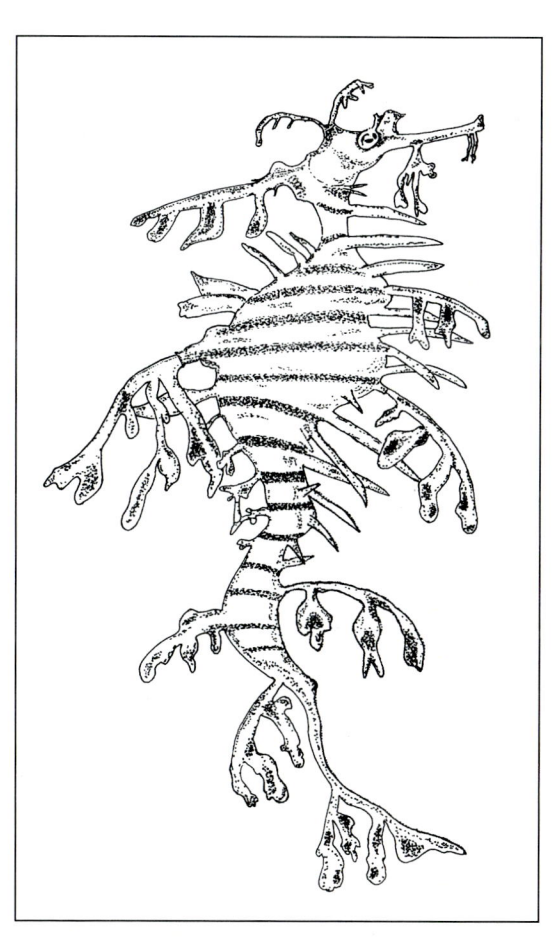

This slow and gentle leafy sea dragon relies on the presence of seaweed for camouflage—it even mimics the plants' movements to avoid detection.

> 2. What must be done to protect sea horses?

Marine Reptiles

Sea turtles, drawn to dense beds of sea grasses, find food and shelter in the bays and lagoons as well. Perfectly adapted to life in the ocean, sea turtles must nonetheless return to land to lay their eggs on sandy beaches (see Chapter 7, Sandy Beaches).

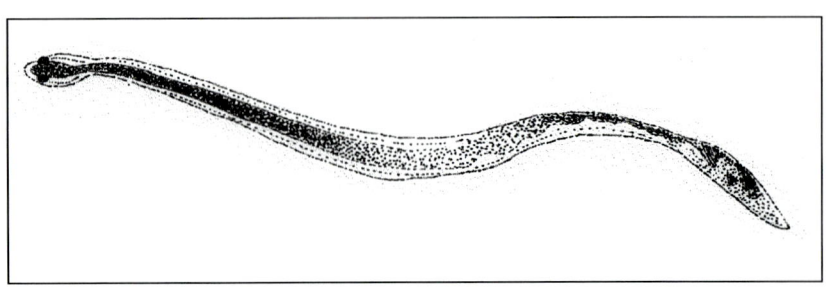

The yellow-bellied sea snake breathes air, but can stay submerged for up to eight hours.

In bays and shallow coastal areas of the southern Pacific Ocean and Indian Ocean, another marine reptile can be found. The sea snake, the ocean's only snake, is a highly venomous coastal dweller. With a flattened, paddlelike tail, the animal efficiently swims through the water. As an air-breathing animal, the sea snake spends much time near the surface around sticks and other floating debris. It is thought that the sea snake hides in the debris waiting for its prey of fish to take shelter there. Large groups of yellow-bellied sea snakes have been observed in such areas. This relative of the cobra carries a venom for stunning prey that is deadly to humans, although attacks are rare and difficult to verify.

Like the sea turtle, young sea snakes develop within eggs and require oxygen from the air to survive. The sea turtle must lay her eggs on shore for them to develop safely, but the sea snake's young develop in eggs within the female's body and are born alive.

> 3. Why is it impossible for sea snake eggs to develop in the water?

Manatees

In the bays and inland waterways of Florida, West Africa, the Caribbean, and the Amazon, a rare and beautiful marine mammal finds a home. The manatee, like the waters in which it lives, is a picture of calm and gentleness. A shy vegetarian, the manatee finds abundant plant life and an absence of aggressive predators in this habitat. It is tolerant of salinity changes and has been known to travel far into freshwater rivers to feed on floating vegetation.

Other than the seasonal movements to warm waters that are required for it to survive, the manatee has no pattern to its life cycle. Young are born at all times of the year after a 13-month gestation period and remain dependent on their mothers for two years. Daily routines center on feeding and frequent naps, which are taken both underwater and floating at the surface.

Manatees interact well with one another and maintain contact with other members of the herd through vocalization, bumping, and mouth contact referred to as kissing.

The West Indian species is commonly called the Florida manatee and ranges into the Caribbean. The West African manatee has been greatly reduced in number in its habitat along the coast of West Africa. The Amazonian manatee remains within the Amazon river basin. The dugong, found in the waters of Australia, has a notched tail fluke and is smaller than the other three species. The Steller's sea cow was a fifth member of the order Sirenia but is now extinct (see Chapter 13, Polar Seas).

The manatee's closest relative is the elephant. The large upper lip of the manatee serves to bring food to the mouth in much the same way an elephant's trunk does. Like the elephant, the manatee also replaces its teeth several times within one lifetime—perhaps because of its herbivorous lifestyle. The tough, leathery skin of the manatee is also similar to that of the elephant.

A young, male Florida manatee confounded scientists and delighted his many admirers in 1995 when his travels northward established new ideas about the manatees' normal home range. Nicknamed Chessie, for the Chesapeake Bay where he was originally captured, fitted with a radio transmitter, and returned to Florida, this young explorer made the same trek the following year. In 1995, Chessie went even farther north to explore Long Island Sound and then Rhode Island before turning around and heading home. Scientists believe manatees may have migrated to the Chesapeake region long ago as part of their normal seasonal activity. Before Chessie's historic trip, Virginia was the most northerly point for manatee sightings.

Some manatees are shy near divers, while others appear curious and come in for a closer look.

Because of their slow, quiet ways, manatees have been widely abused by humans. Traveling slowly through intracoastal waterways, they are frequently struck and killed or injured by boats. Despite strict speed limits in known manatee areas, some are killed each year. Their numbers were originally reduced by hunting. Despite full protection by law, the Florida manatee now numbers only approximately 1,200 individuals. As Florida's human population grows, so also does the threat from pollution, hazardous floating debris, and habitat encroachment. Discarded fishing line has been known to trap and drown manatees, while other deaths occur each year when the animals ingest plastic debris or other harmful pollutants.

Many residents in Florida are committed to protection of the manatee, but still more are unaware of how their activities can harm this endangered animal. Power plants also affect manatee behavior. Warm water from the plants keeps the manatees warm during the winter, as they will quickly die when exposed to cold water. Large groups of manatees can be found near the warm-water vents on cold mornings. These warm-water vents at the power plants may, however, be causing manatees to abandon age-old migratory patterns.

The winter migration of the manatee used to take them to points farther south, without the threat of cold water. Now, when rare cold snaps coincide with power failures in Florida, they lead to many manatee deaths and further endanger the species. No action has yet been taken to prevent the warm water from entering the inland waterway, so the dependence of manatees on the warm water continues.

> 4. Is there any harm in encouraging the manatees to alter their migration patterns? Explain your answer.

Whales

Where manatees find refuge throughout the year in protected waters, a much larger marine mammal uses bays and lagoons only seasonally. The humpback whale travels from polar feeding waters to sheltered lagoons off the coast of Hawaii to mate and bear young. The animals use the warmer water and shelter from open sea hazards to allow their newborn calves to gain strength for the northward migration. As it is only in these lagoons that the famous song of the humpback is heard, the connection between song and mating is undeniable (see Chapter 11, The Open Ocean).

Other whales make a similar migration, although it is much longer and brings the animals close to shore. Gray whales migrate from the Bering Sea where they summer to the lagoons of Baja where they mate and bear their young. This is the longest migration of any mammal: 8,000 kilometers round-trip. Whales seem to use many navigational clues, including landmarks, to find their way. Traveling up and down the Pacific coast of the United States brings the gray whales into close contact with humans, making them the most watched whales in the world. Sightings have become rarer in the last few years, in part because so many whale-watching vessels follow the animals. Many whales are moving farther offshore to prevent these encounters. Guidelines for preventing harassment of the migrating mammals are explicit, but hard to enforce.

> 5. Should whale watching be more closely regulated? Explain.

Scientists have been troubled by a rise in mortality along the gray-whale migration path. Some of the whales that died were clearly malnourished, but others appeared healthy. The unexplained mortality is a blow to whale conservation, especially since the whales' protected status had permitted the population to rebound.

Gray whales may feed in the Baja lagoons as well as the Bering Sea. They are bottom feeders, running their bodies along muddy sediments to stir up small crustaceans that they gulp into their mouths and strain through fringed plates of baleen (see Chapter 11, The Open Ocean). Gray whales stage their annual mating rituals upon reaching the lagoons or as they travel south. Obviously, mating between two 14-meter, 27-metric-ton animals is no easy task. Usually, a sexually mature male is accompanied by a younger male who will assist him in readying the female for courtship and mating.

Once a sexually receptive female is identified, the two males work together to stimulate her. Through a number of dives and rolls the males make constant contact with the female. She is usually shy at first and attempts to dive away. The males pursue until she finally indicates readiness by turning on her back; one male does the same. The whales float side by side at the surface, and the penis of the male is unsheathed and reaches across the body of the female. When the penis makes contact with the female's genital opening, the two whales roll together and the male deposits the sperm. The younger male remains below the female and supports her if needed during copulation. The threesome will travel together for several days before parting company.

The lagoons of Baja have been a favorite destination for whale lovers for many years, as gray whales can be seen in extraordinarily close proximity. Traveling in inflatable boats, humans have the opportunity to see and even touch gray whales. The animals often seem curious about visitors and approach for a closer look; perhaps they are seeking a back rub to remove troublesome barnacles and sea lice that irritate their sensitive skin. This trust is especially remarkable when it is remembered that whalers hunted gray whales in these lagoons until the whales received full protection by law.

Threats to Ecosystems

Shallow bays, lagoons, and inland waterways are vulnerable to pollution from agricultural and industrial runoff, which kills bay grasses and destroys habitats for fish and invertebrates. Nitrogen found in fertilizers promotes blooms of algae, which cause oxygen levels to drop as the algae decomposes. Farmers have asked for federal assistance in modifying agricultural practices to reduce runoff.

As can be seen from the Chesapeake Bay to the Santa Monica Bay, coastal areas are negatively affected by such human activities as overfishing and development. However, other human activities, such as education and conservation, are helpful to coastal ecosystems.

CHAPTER 6 *Subtidal Soft Bottoms*

But always the essence of the lives—the finding of food, the hiding from enemies, the capturing of prey, the producing of young, all that makes up the living and dying and perpetuating—is concealed from the eyes of those who merely glance at the surface of the sand and declare them barren.

RACHEL CARSON

Beyond the sheltered inlets and waterways leading to the sea from the estuary, and extending outward along the continental shelf and margin, is a habitat characterized by sand or mud bottoms. The living things in the subtidal soft-bottom habitat are always submerged. The soft bottoms on and in which they live are exposed to wave action and so are constantly shifting. There are not many species that can survive such instability, but those that can are found in significant numbers. Animals in the subtidal soft-bottom habitat either live in the sediment and are called **infauna** or they live on top of the sediment and are called **epifauna**.

It is impossible for large algae to attach in this habitat, but where sunlight penetrates enough to allow photosynthesis to occur, **diatoms** (DIE a toms) are found on the surface of the sand or mud (see Chapter 11, The Open Ocean). These microscopic protists are eaten by some of the animals, but many more of the animals filter detritus and other suspended particles for food. Invertebrates of this habitat include clams, crabs, moon snails, brittle stars, sea porcupines, and sand dollars. These invertebrates either burrow into the substrate or travel over its surface in search of food.

1. What would the relative absence of plants mean to this habitat?

Invertebrates

The sand dollar has an interesting method of obtaining food in this habitat. Most filter feeders must maintain a current of water through their bodies in order to filter food. Often this water movement is generated by beating cilia—hairs that are capable of moving. The cilia work perfectly to cause this movement, but are limited in strength. The sand dollar uses cilia to create weak movement but also positions itself with its mouth toward the prevailing current. It therefore has a greater chance of encountering wave-borne food, which it then transports to its mouth along mucus-covered grooves.

Sand dollars, which live in large numbers in many parts of the world, are frequently tossed ashore after storms.

2. What is required for a filter-feeding animal to orient itself toward prevailing currents?

The subtidal soft bottoms, along with many other habitats, are home to some of the marine worms. Unlike terrestrial worms, marine worms can be brightly colored and many have delicate, graceful bodies. Although the ocean supports many different worm species, here in the subtidal soft bottom the **polychaete** (POL i keet) worms are the dominant group.

Polychaete worms are placed in the phylum Annelida with the leech and earthworm because all are segmented. Each segment contains a pair of **parapodia**—flattened appendages that together with bristlelike **setae** (SE tee) assist the animal in moving. The setae give these worms their name: the word *polychaeta* means "many bristles." The head, called the prostomium, contains light- and chemo-sensitive organs that allow the worm to gather information from its environment as it moves. The prostomium makes up the first two segments of the worm's body and contains the mouth, two pairs of eyes, three antennae, several tentacles, and a pair of palps (tiny organs used in feeding). The segmented body of the polychaete worms allows for great variation in form, habitat, and feeding strategies.

clam worm Nereis

lug worm Avenicola

fan worm Sabella

blood worm Glycera

ornate worm Amphitrite

The marine segmented worms exhibit great structural diversity. Among them are these five genuses of polychaetes: Amphitrite, Avenicola, Glycera, Nereis, *and* Sabella.

> 3. For each polychaete above, explain whether the worm is part of the infauna or epifauna. What is it about each animal that leads you to your conclusion?

Polychaetes exhibit one of three feeding strategies. Suspension feeding is performed by the fan worms known as feather duster worms and Christmas tree worms. Their spiraling radioles (small, feathery structures) gather food and oxygen from the water. These worms are also found in coral reef-habitats. An example of a polychaete that carries out deposit feeding is the lug worm, which uses mucus-coated tentacles to gather food from the sediment. Raptorial feeding, or the capturing of prey with hooklike jaws, is exhibited by the bloodworm. This polychaete is highly mobile and swims freely or burrows within sediments.

> 4. Which food-gathering strategy seems to take advantage of a segmented body?
>
> 5. Why are fan worms better suited for the coral-reef habitat than for the subtidal habitat?

Vertebrates

Subtidal soft bottoms are ideally suited for certain invertebrates, but also have a few interesting vertebrate visitors. The sand dab, a relative of the flounder, is a curious fish that has a fascinating method of dealing with life in the soft-bottom habitat. This flat fish spends most of its time lying flat on the sand, unseen by predators and prey. Perfectly camouflaged, it has special pigment cells known as **chromatophores** (crow MA toe fours), which change size, shape, and position to match the substrate. The sand dab, class Osteichthyes, also partially buries itself with a light dusting of sand. Seeing from this position is no problem for the sand dab, because as it matures one eye migrates to join the other eye on one side of the body.

The sand dab changes its coloration to blend in with the ocean floor.

Cartilaginous fish, class **Chondrichthyes** (con DRIK theez), are well represented in the subtidal soft-bottom habitat. Skates, smaller versions of rays, find their flattened bodies are suited to epifaunal life. They travel through these habitats, filtering suspended material for food. Southern stingrays are also common in these areas. Their sting is widely feared, but the animal will only sting when stepped on. The angel shark, a shy member of this class, spends time on the soft bottom, although its strange migration patterns are not yet fully understood. The animal has been known to lie dormant for many days and then to travel many kilometers within a single night.

> 6. Name one member of the infauna and one member of the epifauna in this habitat.
>
> 7. Compare and contrast life in the estuary with life in the subtidal soft bottoms.

CHAPTER 7 *Sandy Beaches*

To stand at the edge of the sea . . . is to have knowledge of things that are as eternal as any earthly life can be.

Rachel Carson

For hundreds of millions of years, waves have encountered the shallows of land and have risen to break against countless beaches. The land, however, cannot withstand the force of the water and the gradual but inevitable process of erosion has taken its toll. The land yields to the pounding of the sea, sand shifts, and rocks are exposed. But the sea gives back some of what it washes away in its subtle seasonal cycles. The year's storms and the following calm bring changes to our shorelines which are often quite dramatic. This cycle of building and washing away maintains the world's sandy beaches.

Sandy Beaches of the United States

The coasts of the United States feature a great diversity of sandy beaches. Some lie on the borders of the continent where the continental shelf causes a gradual breaking of waves. Others border islands where no such shelf exists. Here the breakers can be quite violent, rolling through miles of open sea before breaking abruptly against the islands. Some of the beaches formed slowly, the years of pounding sea against corals, rocks, and shells causing the deposition of sand particles. Others, such as the black sand beaches of Hawaii, formed quickly when hot lava from a volcanic eruption reached the sea.

Although our beaches vary greatly, the life forms that exist on them remain quite similar. The sandy beach is home to few animals, but many feed or breed there. Most animals that live out their lives on the beach are invertebrates; crabs in particular have found great success there. Sand crabs burrowing in the moist sand are prey to many species of shore birds. Ghost crabs scurry about on the dry sand, finding that a nocturnal, scavenging lifestyle on the darkened beaches suits their shy natures. They dwell on the beach in burrows and can remain out of the water for long periods of time. Mole crabs burrow within the surf zone, where they are harvested by many species of birds. Tiny sand hoppers are typically found beneath moist seaweed washed ashore. Clams burrow in the sand as well, although most species prefer the nutrient-rich sediment of mudflats within estuaries.

> 1. How would a sand crab in Florida differ from a sand crab in Hawaii?
>
> 2. Why does the sandy beach provide a good habitat for crabs?
>
> 3. Why would this habitat be difficult for most animals?

The sandy beach is an active, changing place: it has been and continues to be the site of dramatic activity. It was on the sandy beach that the first life form to venture from the sea probably walked. Like the evasive ghost crab, this ancient adventurer was probably an arthropod initially leaving the sea for only short periods of time and returning to the surf to oxygenate its gills. Biologists theorize that this event took place approximately 400 million years ago, beginning the colonization of the land.

> 4. What might motivate an animal to leave the sea for a hostile beach?

A Site for Reproduction

Although the appearance of the first marine animal on the beach so many millions of years ago is noteworthy, other species still leave the relative safety of the sea to deposit their eggs on shore. Born with an ancient instinct to leave their young on land, these animals make annual treks onto beaches and then return once their reproductive obligation is completed.

Grunion, a small bony fish, come ashore in mass mating runs to lay eggs above the year's highest tide line. Leaping out of the waves to dig a hole for her eggs, the female waits for a male (or several males) to encircle her. Egg and sperm are released simultaneously into the nest. The male immediately hops into the next wave and is returned to the sea. The female secures the nest with her tail fin before taking a wave to safety.

> 5. What is the advantage of laying eggs out of the water? What are the disadvantages?

Although they spend their entire lives in the ocean, sea turtles return to sandy beaches to lay their eggs. Air-breathing, they are one of the sea's few reptiles whose shelled egg and watertight skin make them ideally suited for terrestrial life. For sea turtles, it is the shelled egg that demands that the nest be made on land. The pores in the shell allow for gas exchange: oxygen from the air is delivered to the embryo while carbon dioxide from its respiration escapes. If these eggs were laid in water, the embryo within would drown. The return to land for the nesting process is the greatest strain to an adult sea turtle.

Shore birds feed on insects and other invertebrates in the sand.

Females make the long march up the beach to lay eggs in a nest dug in the sand. Using her flipperlike forelimbs, which have been modified for sea life, the

The green turtle is found in shallow coastal waters.

female pulls herself up the beach and digs the nest one meter into the cool, moist sand. She must carefully choose a nest site above the high-tide line, because her offspring will die if exposed to salt water before hatching. As with many other reptiles, the temperature of the nest will determine the gender of the turtles.

Up to 100 eggs incubate for 30 days before the hatchlings emerge to make the long and dangerous trip down the beach to the sea. The hatchlings instinctively move toward light. Some are tricked by street lights when they emerge at night and become lost or exhausted before reaching the relative safety of the sea. Even at night they are susceptible to many predators for whom they are easy prey. Most emerge at sunrise after the sand in which they are buried becomes slightly warmed. The hatchlings race toward the sea's edge, pulling themselves through the sand with flippers, which at this point in their development are as long as their bodies. They face aquatic predators once within the sea, but at least there they are more agile and better able to conceal themselves than on the open beaches.

> 6. What can be done to prevent turtles from moving toward lights near the beach?

Sea turtles return to the same stretch of beach on which they were born to lay their own eggs. The mechanism they use to identify the beach is still a mystery, but some biologists theorize that the animals smell the sand as they travel from nest to ocean after hatching. **Imprinting** on the beach in this way, sea turtles can identify their "home" beach and return there to mate and nest when sexually mature.

> 7. Why must a sea turtle leave its eggs on land for them to develop?
>
> 8. What is the most vulnerable point in a sea turtle's life?

Some sea turtle species mate at the same approximate time and lay their eggs on the same beach in a huge gathering known as mass nesting. Adults time mating and the laying of eggs so that young emerge together, hundreds of hatchlings traveling from the nest to the sea at the same time. Olive and Kemp's Ridley sea turtles nest this way.

> 9. What are the advantages and disadvantages of mass nesting?
>
> 10. During reproduction, what additional stress is placed on the grunion that is not placed on the sea turtle?

Threats to Sea Turtles

Humans pose a threat to sea turtle populations, endangering nearly all sea turtle species. Fishers drown large numbers of air-breathing turtles in their trawling nets while attempting to capture shrimp. Turtle Exclusion Devices (TEDs) are trapdoors within the nets which allow trapped turtles to exit safely; they are required by law in the United States. The United States banned the import of shrimp from countries that do not require TEDs, but, in a blow to the global effort to protect sea turtles, the World Trade Organization has ruled against the ban.

Sea turtles are also sought for food and for products made from their shells. The developing embryos of sea turtles are considered a delicacy in Japan, and in the Caribbean, sea turtles are killed for meat and leather.

Some sea turtles feed on sea jellies, which places them in still more danger. Plastic bags floating in the water resemble jellies. Sea turtles have been known to feed on the plastic and may either choke as they attempt to swallow or starve to death as their stomachs become filled with indigestible debris. Sea turtles have been found dead or dying of starvation with stomachs full of plastic bags. No plastics should ever be thrown from a boat.

Sea turtles are easily discouraged from coming ashore for the stressful work of nesting. Light and other signs of human activity prevent the shy reptiles from choosing a nesting site. Often turtles return to the beaches where they were born only to find them developed and therefore unacceptable for nesting.

It is important for individuals who are committed to sea turtle preservation to avoid products that might directly or indirectly support endangering practices.

Birds and Mammals of the Beach

Several bird species search for food along sandy beaches and within the mudflats of estuaries. Most are equipped with legs and beaks that are designed to exploit very specific food.

> 11. Carefully study the beaks and bodies of the birds on the next page. For each, describe what part of the beach it is likely to visit to find food.

ruddy turnstone

sanderling

willet

Marine mammals are sometimes found on sandy beaches. Some pinnipeds, for example (see Chapter 8, Rocky Shores), return to breeding beaches each year where males fight over females and pups learn to swim in shallow water. It is on beaches such as this in Patagonia (a remote region on the southeastern coast of South America) that orcas leap from the water onto the sand to snatch unwary sea lion pups.

Several marine mammals make their way to sandy beaches when ill—sea otters, pinnipeds, and even whales and dolphins. When whales and dolphins "beach" (as the stranding behavior is called), they are placed in great danger because of their tremendous weight. Accustomed to the buoyancy provided by ocean water, they can be crushed by their own weight when beached. Their skin is also very sensitive and therefore susceptible to sunburn and drying. Time in the sun is painful and dangerous.

Many studies are being conducted to determine the cause of these strandings; explanations vary, but none of them is conclusive. The animals may beach when they are ill and unable to continue swimming, they may be responding to the alarm calls of ill members of their **pod,** or they may be disoriented by an internal parasite or an unusual magnetism interfering with their ability to navigate. All are possibilities that require further study.

The most unusual strandings have involved seemingly healthy animals that did nothing to free themselves. In one particular incident, the largest adult in a pod of pilot whales, an obviously ill male, was beached and sending alarm signals. All other members of the pod were either beached or were free-floating just a few feet from shore and did not appear to be ill. These whales—most of them females, their young, and adolescent males—would not leave the beach, nor would they swim away when led by volunteers or freed by the incoming tide. After three days of this puzzling behavior, the large male died. At that time volunteers were successful in leading the whales from the beach into the open sea. Possible explanations for this behavior are most intriguing.

> 12. Why do you think the apparently healthy whales refused to leave the distressed male on the beach?

Threats to Beach Ecosystems

For centuries humans have flocked to the sea's edge to recreate and to build homes. The inevitable change that has followed is in many ways not an improvement. Loss of wildlife habitat, erosion, littering, sewage spills, and toxic runoff all have the potential to alter and damage our beaches irreversibly. The use of hard stabilization, structures to hold the beach in place, is widely criticized because it prevents the natural ebb and flow of sand (see Chapter 3, Islands).

Dunes are also an important part of the sandy beach habitat. Supporting grasses and other vegetation are held in place, preventing erosion. In areas where the dunes have been disturbed (primarily through development), beaches and inland properties lose sand. The resulting rising sea levels make erosion problems more severe, as grasses are killed when exposed to too much salt water.

The northern elephant seal uses sandy beaches such as these at Piedras Blancas in San Luis Obispo, California, to mate and bear their young.

13. What must be done so that we can enjoy the beach, but also be certain it will remain for future generations?

Many citizens volunteer their time for adopt-a-beach programs that are designed to keep beaches clear of hazardous debris. Plastics, polystyrene (Styrofoam®) products, and medicinal garbage have been making their way to our beaches in record quantities. Keeping beaches clean and free of debris makes them more pleasant for visitors and safer for the other animals who spend time there. Walking the adopted beach regularly and removing debris also helps to develop a spirit of protection and a sense of pride in "ownership." It encourages intelligent treatment of one of the oceans' great gifts to us—the sandy beach.

Dune grass stabilizes the natural beach-dune complex.

SANDY BEACHES   59

CHAPTER 8 *Rocky Shores*

*Earth and Ocean seem
To sleep in one another's
   arms and dream
Of waves, flowers,
   clouds, woods, rocks,
   and all that we
Read in their smiles
   and call reality.*

PERCY BYSSHE SHELLEY

While the substrata of the estuaries, sandy beaches, subtidal soft bottoms, and shallow bays are soft and shifting, those of the rocky shores could not be more solid. On the rugged, rocky coasts and offshore all the way to the continental margin where reefs occur, animals and plants adapted for life on the rocks have evolved a number of clinging mechanisms. Claws, muscular feet, tubes, adhesives, and scraping devices all help to assure survival in a habitat where competition for space is a daily hardship. Within the intertidal zone, where rocks are exposed to wave action, the pounding surf and changing tide demand that plants and animals withstand additional pressures.

Invertebrates on the Rocky Shore

One animal that finds a home in this rocky habitat is the aggregating anemone. Growing in large groups along rock surfaces, these cnidarians filter feed at high tide. Their "grouping" behavior may prevent water loss from individual anemones. Most anemones in the group have been formed by fission (splitting to form two genetically identical individuals). Often large bands of rock uninhabited by anemones can be found between genetically dissimilar groups. If an anemone comes into contact with the tentacles of a "stranger," it will swell and attack the newcomer with stinging cells. Often the victim will pull back or dislodge itself from the rock to be carried away by a wave. Anemones will tolerate touching the tentacles of relatives.

These aggregating anemones grow in large groups on rock surfaces.

1. Why do anemones attack unrelated competitors but not relatives, when there is competition for food among all anemones?
2. Why might aggregating prevent water loss?

Large clumps of mussels (phylum Mollusca) use byssal threads and a remarkable adhesive to cling to rock surfaces. These animals filter food from the water surrounding them at high tide and clamp tightly shut to avoid water loss at low tide.

3. Why are mussels ideally suited for life on the rocky shores?

Sea stars (phylum Echinodermata) are found in the company of mussels, their main prey in many areas. Although slow and seemingly harmless, the sea star is a formidable predator. Its tube feet, characteristic of all echinoderms, clamp tightly onto the shells of bivalves and pull them slightly open. The sea star then everts its stomach (it comes out of the body) and digests the mussel right in its own shell.

Large colonies of mussels seem to have a line beyond which they cannot grow. Toward the high tide line, that boundary is determined by exposure to the air; mussels cannot tolerate long periods of time out of the water, so they do not colonize these areas. Sea stars can tolerate less time out of the water than the mussels can, so they are not able to move as far toward the shore to feed. The sea star is too slow to return safely from mussel beds to deeper water before the tide recedes. Sea stars instead graze on the mussels that are found farther out in the water, creating the lower boundary of the mussel bands.

Limpets (phylum Mollusca) have a strong muscular foot with which to cling to rock surfaces. They are so effective in scraping algae from the rocks with a structure known as a radula that they sometimes also carve out a hole for themselves into which they retreat at low tide. Periwinkles, tiny black-shelled gastropods, are often found in the company of limpets and behave in a similar way. Mussels, limpets, and periwinkles all face the rigors of high and low tide.

Mussels, sea stars, and sea urchins share this rocky habitat.

A Pacific rocky shore invertebrate known as the owl limpet carries its taste for algae one step further than its smaller relatives. This animal farms algae by maintaining a 30-centimeter by 30-centimeter grazing territory known as a home scar. The owl limpet patrols this area grazing on algae, but it leaves behind an algal turf: rough growth on which new algae will quickly sprout. Smaller limpets and other grazers will scrape away all algae including the algal turf, which makes it necessary for them to move to new grazing areas. Some owl limpets have been known to remain on the same home scar for four years.

4. What are the advantages of maintaining a home scar?

Not only does the owl limpet care for its algae to encourage growth, but this ambitious invertebrate also keeps other animals from encroaching on its territory. Using a variety of behaviors the limpet "persuades" unwanted guests to depart from its home scar.

When faced by other smaller limpets, the owl limpet backs up its own shell and pushes against the intruder's shell until it is dislodged. To eliminate the

Sea stars are able to regenerate body parts. If a ray is severed, the animal simply grows a new one.

ROCKY SHORES 63

Limpets generally feed by grazing on algal growths on rocks.

The barnacle uses a cement gland to attach itself to rocks, shells, ship bottoms, and other submerged objects.

The adult sea squirt is sessile, or permanently attached to a surface.

threat from mussels and barnacles, the owl limpet scrapes away their adhesive threads, like a small plow, to make it impossible for them to stay attached to the rock surface. When it encounters a snail, the owl limpet raises its shell and then drops it quickly, catching a portion of the snail's muscular foot. The snail will attempt to retreat into its shell and at this point the limpet releases its hold, causing the snail to be carried away by the next wave.

5. How might a biologist study these behaviors?

Some crabs also find food, shelter, and mates in this rocky habitat. Shore crabs and rock crabs are able to do quite well scurrying in and out of rock crevices scavenging for food. Like most other crabs, they are able to tolerate time away from the water, needing only to reoxygenate their gills periodically with a quick dip in a passing wave.

Polychaete worms also do well in rocky habitats, some growing to be a meter long. In deeper water, rock reefs are covered with clinging invertebrate life forms: anemones, crabs, hydroids, sponges, and worms all grow in beautiful underwater gardens. Nibbling fish live nearby to reap the harvest.

The pilings of piers and wharfs provide living space for rocky-shore invertebrates, as the solid surface resembles their traditional habitats. The free swimming larvae settle on the wood pilings just as they would on rocks. Some, such as barnacles, are called fouling organisms because they cling to and "foul" the underside of boats. Barnacles are found in a number of marine habitats. Some encrust on pilings or rocks while others burrow into the skin of whales. Classified as arthropods, barnacles cement their heads to a solid surface and gather food with their feet.

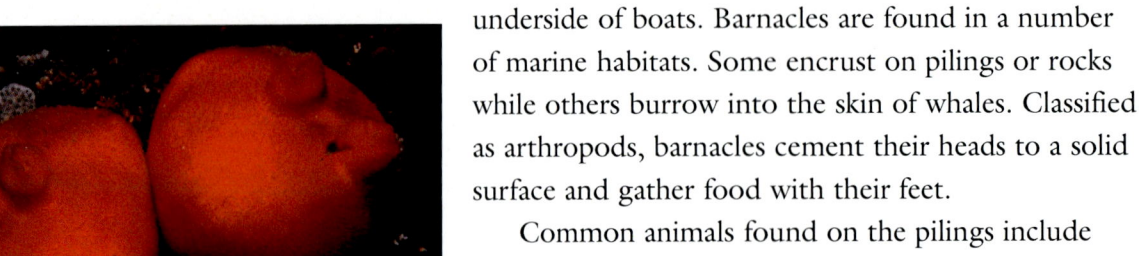

Common animals found on the pilings include anemones, sponges, and sea squirts. Sea squirts are placed in the phylum Vertebrata, despite their soft-bodied adult forms. Sea squirts have, as larvae, a primitive backbone known as a notochord. In one species, the free-swimming larva has a rudimentary brain. After settling and beginning life as an adult, it no longer needs the brain and eats it. Scientists are

64   MARINE BIOLOGY

studying how these sessile animals communicate with each other on the rocks, where competition for space is intense.

The coasts of deep ocean islands are frequently rocky. Their location, far away from the continental shelf, causes waves breaking against the rocks of these islands to be particularly fierce. Few rocky shores are more inhospitable than those of the Galápagos Islands. Here in the crashing surf of the Pacific, on the sharp volcanic rock, the world's only marine lizard is able to survive.

> 6. Why would an island experience stronger wave action than a continental coastline?

Reptiles and Birds of the Rocky Shore

The marine iguana, a reptile and a direct ancestor of the mainland green iguana, is a vegetarian that feeds exclusively on algae. Using sharply-clawed feet, it clings to rock surfaces, withstanding pounding surf to feed. Marine iguanas are frequently found in large groups basking on the black volcanic rock to raise their body temperatures after dipping into the chilly Pacific Ocean waters to feed.

> 7. Why are reptiles such unlikely marine inhabitants?
>
> 8. Why must marine iguanas raise their body temperatures after spending time in the water to feed?

Marine iguanas differ from terrestrial iguanas in a number of interesting ways. They have blunt snouts that allow them to graze on algae very close to rock surfaces. They are able to remove excess salt from their bodies through their nasal passages. Most importantly, they are able to remain underwater to feed for extended periods of time—up to 30 minutes. They have been seen feeding as far as 400 meters from shore. This lizard is a true evolutionary wonder and allows us a glimpse of the adaptations a species must make to a hostile environment such as the rocky shore.

Throughout the world, ocean rocks are commonly used by various seabirds as resting spots or for nesting. Steep rock faces or remote, rocky islands provide seabirds with shelter from terrestrial predators and direct access to fishing waters. Such forbidding nesting sites might increase offsprings' chances for survival.

Puffins nest along rocky coasts and on islands in the northern oceans. They spend much of their time "flying" underwater hunting small fish.

ROCKY SHORES 65

Favorites among birders (individuals who enjoy watching birds), the Atlantic, horned, and tufted puffins nest on rocky shores. Laying their eggs either on rock outcroppings or within burrows of soil along cliffs, the puffins raise their young as "cliff hangers."

Male and female puffins cooperate in rearing their young and take turns seeking their prey of small fish in the water below the nest. Protected from terrestrial predators, the chicks will be unmolested until they fly off on their own. Adult puffins, on the other hand, are constantly harassed by gulls and other aggressive birds.

Puffins fish until their large, colorful beaks are full and then return to the nest to feed either their chicks or their mates. Gulls take advantage of this "beakful" of food and frighten the shy puffins with raucous dives and other threatening displays. Shocked by this aggression, the puffin opens its beak and the fish fall. The gull immediately drops and consumes the stolen prey. More prey will be lost to gulls than will ever reach their young, so the adult puffins must work very hard to keep their hungry chicks well fed.

Atlantic puffins are found only in coastal Maine and Canada; the horned and tufted puffins are found in small numbers in southeast Alaska. Auks, guillemots (GIL eh mots), kittiwakes (KIT ee wakes), murrelets (MER lits), murres (mers), and razorbills also nest along rocky shores.

9. Why might a bird such as the puffin nest on rocky shores of islands?

Mammals of the Rocky Shore

There is one group of marine mammals that frequents rocky shores—the pinnipeds, or seals and sea lions. Of all the marine mammals, the pinnipeds most clearly show their link with land. Pinniped means feather-footed and it is these fins that allow the animals (especially sea lions) mobility on land and in the water. Graceful and acrobatic in the water where they hunt for fish, they are slow and awkward on the land where they bask in the sun and bear young.

Seals and sea lions probably prefer rocky shores because of their isolation and rugged protection from terrestrial predators. When pursued by aquatic predators such as great white sharks, the rocks provide hasty retreats.

Fur seals must spend time each day grooming to keep their hair free of mats.

Seals and sea lions differ from one another in a number of ways. Sea lions are known as eared seals because they have a visible external ear flap; seals lack this ear flap. Sea lions also tend to be more social and more intelligent than seals. Sea lions can support their weight on their front flippers and so are able to raise themselves up on land and "walk." The rear flippers can move forward and backward, contributing to the animals' ability to move successfully on land. The seal is always "belly down" on land, so these animals must always "caterpillar crawl" to move.

All pinniped mothers draw heavily on fat reserves to produce one of nature's richest milks for their young.

10. Name the differences between seals and sea lions.

Threats to Rocky-Shore Ecosystems

Seals and sea lions were hunted for their fur in many areas. The pups of some species have unusually soft fur, so they were the main hunting target. Hunters killed the pups as they lay beside their helpless mothers on the ice or rocky shores of their summer breeding and pupping grounds. Such furs still sell as luxury items.

Groups interested in seal fishing have worked hard to bring an end to the legal annual hunting of harp seal pups, but because the furs sell, some pups are killed each year by poachers.

11. What is your view on the use of animal furs for luxury items?

Although heavily preyed upon by sharks, pinnipeds face their greatest competition from humans. As the commercial fishing industry takes more and more fish from the ocean, pinnipeds will continue to be viewed as rivals. Under the Federal Marine Mammal Protection Act of 1972, pinnipeds are protected, but commercial fishers are authorized to use nonlethal measures including shooting at or near a seal or sea lion considered a threat to fishing gear.

Many recreational fishers believe a connection exists between the rise in the pinniped population and the decline of salmon populations. It is true that some pinnipeds (the Steller sea lion in particular) have been seen near fish ladders, devices designed to assist salmon in navigating dams. However, the worldwide depletion of fish stocks, including salmon, is most likely the result of overfishing.

12. What type of data would demonstrate that seals and sea lions are causing the decline in fish populations?

CHAPTER 9 *Tide Pools*

It is advisable to look from the tide pool to the stars and then back to the tide pool again.

JOHN STEINBECK

Closely associated with the rocky shore is another unique marine habitat—the tide pool. In rock depressions within the intertidal zone where pools of water collect, a hardy group of creatures lives and thrives. Pounded at high tide and left to heat up in the pools at low tide, the life forms of the tide pools show great tenacity and specialization for life in this wet, rocky world. The Pacific coast of the United States provides many areas for studying these unique habitats.

Living Conditions in the Tide-Pool Ecosystem

A tide pool on the coast of Maine. A rich diversity of life can be found in this "world between the tides."

With the ebb and flow of the tide come dramatic changes for tide-pool life. Changes in oxygen, pH, salinity, and temperature are more extreme here than in any other marine habitat. The isolation of low tide, when no water enters these pools, is the time of greatest change; when this occurs during daylight, fluctuations are intensified. The water temperature can rise as much as 15 degrees Celsius. Salinity can change from 35 ppm (parts per million) to 45 ppm as water evaporates in the bright sunlight, leaving salts behind. During the day, plants and plant-like protists of the tide pools carry out photosynthesis, releasing dissolved oxygen into their pools. The pools at low tide become acidic from the presence of excess carbon dioxide given off by animal respiration.

1. Why would a midday low tide be particularly difficult for organisms living in a tide pool?

2. Why is dissolved carbon dioxide more concentrated in tide pools at low tide?

When the tide returns, it restores "normal" pH, salinity, and temperature and carries with it dissolved oxygen, plankton, and other nutrients to nourish and freshen the tide pools. Wastes that would poison the pools if left too long are also washed away. But this rescue comes with a price—the brutal wave action of the intertidal zone. Large or deep tide pools do not experience the extreme changes to which small or shallow ones are susceptible. The greatest variety of life occurs in the tide pools that are lowest in the intertidal zone. Less affected by low tide, they do not experience the wide fluctuations of those pools found on higher ground.

Algae in Tide Pools

Despite the seemingly impossible living conditions within these pools of water, life is plentiful: an endless array of protists, plants, and animals crowd the tide pools, making them appear like beautiful coastal gardens. Many of these colors and textures are due to the interesting algae that make their homes there.

Like many animals, algae must have structures that allow them to attach in their pools and withstand heavy wave action. One organism that has accomplished both of these objectives is the coralline algae. Composed of calcium carbonate, whose strength gives greater protection from the waves, this algae can be either encrusting (growing flat against the rock) or articulated (forming short branching structures). Attached in great profusion, the coralline algae's ability to withstand exposure to the waves is key to its success in this habitat. Its many shades of pastel pink add beauty to tide pools.

Another organism, called spongeweed or dead men's fingers, also finds the tide pool an appropriate habitat. Its spongy texture gives it the look of fingers, which led to both its common names.

Red algae can also be found growing in the tide pools. It gives shelter to some animals with its short, dense **blades** and is food to others. It occurs in hues of deep red and purple. Occasionally, blades of the giant kelp make their way into the tide pools where they provide both food and shelter to the animals living there.

The mouth of this giant green anemone is in the center of the oral disk, surrounded by delicate tentacles.

3. In what ways do algae benefit the tide-pool ecosystem?

Other tide-pool organisms have such intriguing common names as delicate-veined violet rockweed, iridescent seaweed, ruffled purple rockweed, sea felt, and sea lettuce. These plants provide beauty, color, and contrast to their tide-pool homes.

Invertebrates in the Tide-Pool Ecosystem

Although it was long mistaken as a plant because of its greenish tinge and flowery appearance, the giant green anemone is an animal. Leading a sessile (stationary) life in the tide pools, this member of the phylum Cnidaria stings its small prey and draws them into its central mouth for digestion. The green color comes from the presence of single-celled green algae that find shelter in the anemone's flowing tentacles. Anemones are able to move, using primitive muscle contractions, but most giant green anemones do not. They are aptly named: these simple animals can grow to be 25 centimeters across.

> 4. Name an animal in another marine habitat that was long mistaken for a plant. What aspect of modern taxonomy prevents such errors?

Tube worm cases

Another cnidarian that has appeared in other habitats is the hydroid. This simple animal is actually a colony of polyps, each one specialized for a different function—defense, feeding, or reproduction. These animals reproduce by forming reproductive polyps called gonozooids, which will break away and swim freely as medusas (mouth and tentacles face downward). When mature, the medusas will release egg and sperm, which will hopefully unite to form a zygote. This will develop into a primitive free-swimming larva, which will finally settle and grow into a new adult colony of polyps.

Examples of hydroids that live in the tide pools include the brown bushy hydroid, brilliant orange hydroid, purple hydrocoral, and ostrich plume hydroid.

The tide pools also support rich populations of worms. Like those shown above, many build tubes for support while others burrow into the sand at the base of the pools and use long feeding tentacles to gather food.

> 5. How do tubes help the worms deal with low-tide exposure, as in the picture above?

Other worms, like the sand castle worm, live together in beautiful colonies. The colony begins with just a few worms building their tubes on rock faces. Eventually their numbers grow and they form large structures with a combination of sand and mucus.

> 6. What type of site would allow a successful worm colony to grow?

Members of the phylum Mollusca also have their representatives in the tide pools. Numerous species of limpet, mussel, nudibranch, sea slug, and snail join one of the largest and most interesting of tide pool mollusks, the sea hare. This large invertebrate has a reduced shell: only a small remnant remains beneath the fleshy mantle. Despite the absence of a shell, the sea hare has an effective defensive behavior. When alarmed or frightened, it will release a cranberry-colored fluid and mucus to discourage offenders.

The sea hare moves through the tide pools grazing on algae, unlike its nudibranch cousins, which feed on other small animals (sponges and hydroids). Its gills appear along the dorsal side of the body within two simple folds. To reproduce, a sea hare mates with another member of its species, although it has no need for dramatic courtship displays to find a proper mate. As hermaphrodites, the animals carry both male and female organs; both will mate to exchange sperm and then both will lay eggs in a spiraling cluster or flat sheet (depending on the species). Once hatched, the zygotes are free-swimming before they settle on a solid surface to mature into adult animals.

A "sand castle" begins like this: A few worms build their sand-and-mucus cases on a rock to begin a colony.

7. What are some of the advantages gained by the sea hare as a result of being hermaphroditic?

The abundant protist, plant, and animal life and many crevices for hiding make the tide pools and their surrounding rocky shores ideal habitats for members of the phylum Arthropoda. Shrimps and crabs scurrying about are among the most mobile of tide-pool invertebrates; they must be quick because they are heavily preyed upon by birds and fish.

One of the arthropods of the tide pool is the hermit crab. It is a member of the class Crustacea, but unlike its tough-shelled relatives, the hermit crab has a soft abdomen; only its claws are armored. It must find suitable shelter to protect its vulnerable abdomen or be easy prey to any number of predators. Black turban snail shells are the shelter of choice for most hermit crabs, although they will use even the abandoned cases of tube worms. Competition for the shells is intense, as the crabs must move to a new one when they outgrow the old. Appearing in large populations in the tide pools, they can be easily watched as they move about on the bottom scavenging for bits of food.

The sea hare gets its name from its prominent tentacles, which resemble rabbit ears.

TIDE POOLS 73

The sea spider, another arthropod, is sometimes found with the great green sea anemone. A delicate-legged animal, it sometimes feeds on the soft tissues of the anemone as it hides beneath it for protection. Some sea spiders can also be found camouflaged among hydroid colonies or within rock crevices.

> 8. What type of symbiosis is the relationship between the sea spider and the great green sea anemone?

Echinoderms have also found great success in the tide pools. In addition to the several sea star species, which were mentioned in some detail in Chapter 8 (Rocky Shores), tide pools also provide homes to brittle stars, sea cucumbers, and a number of different sea urchins. Brittle stars are so named because they have the ability to sever their own rays in a contracting behavior known as autotomy (self-cut). This allows them to escape a predator by leaving behind the bit of ray, which they can then regenerate. One of the meekest of echinoderms, the brittle star burrows in the soft sand on the floor of tide pools and extends its long rays to gather small prey.

Sea cucumbers can be found in several habitats—they find success from the rocky intertidal zone to the deep ocean.

Sea cucumbers are found in nearly every habitat, including the tide pools. They feed on plankton, using one of two food-gathering strategies. They either filter-feed with an extravagant branched feeding apparatus, or they use mucus-coated oral tube feet to move plankton to their mouth. Sea cucumbers all gather oxygen with a structure known as a respiratory tree, which is found just inside the anus (all sea cucumbers have two body openings). For defense, the leathery animal will eviscerate, or expel, its digestive organs, which will stick to the attacker and repel it. The sticky mucus-covered organs will then regenerate.

Like the sea cucumber, the sea urchin uses its tube feet to attach to rock surfaces in the tide pools. Protected by its battery of spines, this echinoderm moves about slowly, feeding on algae and small invertebrates. In some areas, sea urchins scrape away a scar in the rock in which they reside. Some remain in the scar permanently; their food comes to them with the tide. Others remain within the sheltered scars only for short periods. The giant red urchin and purple urchin are commonly found in the tide pools.

Most sculpin are found in shallow sea waters, though some live in deeper waters, or even freshwater.

Fish of the Tide Pool

Like the many invertebrates that make their homes in the tide pools, a few fish find that the secluded pools make ideal shelters; some come into the tide pools as juveniles in order to avoid larger predators offshore. Feeding on plankton and small invertebrates, these fish gain strength and size for life offshore. Several species of blenny and sculpin (SKULL pin) live in the tide pools as do juvenile opaleye (a kelp forest species).

> 9. What aspects of the tide-pool ecosystem are advantageous to juvenile fish?
>
> 10. What rigors do these fish endure that are not faced by those species found offshore?

Threats to Tide-Pool Ecosystems

Tide pools are easily accessible to anyone interested in observing the life of the sea in action. They may be the only place in the wild where a nonswimmer can see and touch a marine organism in its natural habitat.

When people enter the tide pools with no knowledge of their impact, damage is inevitable. Tide pools now suffer from being loved too much. Every foot that steps into a tide pool steps on something alive, probably crushing it. No habitat can withstand this type of trampling; even the largest, most powerful waves at high tide are small compared to an ill-placed foot. Often, in their eagerness to see or touch an animal or plant, people pry it from its attachment point, sometimes killing it. Rocks overturned to find what hides beneath them can fatally shadow the algae growing on top. Overcollecting has further devastated these areas. Destruction on an even larger scale from sewage and oil spills threatens tide pools. Development along the coast continues to disrupt native terrestrial plant populations near tide pools. Where few plants remain, soil and silt flow to the sea, smothering some of the few remaining pristine tide-pool areas. Despite its strength and tenacity for life in a world of changes between the tides, the tide-pool ecosystem needs our protection.

Pristine tide pools such as these in Portuguese Bend, California, are increasingly rare due to the pressures of coastal development.

> 11. How should potential damage to tide pools factor into coastal development plans?

TIDE POOLS

CHAPTER 10 *Kelp Forests*

I was taken out in a little boat . . . then after about five minutes we came to the kelp beds, those extraordinary seaweed beds that are so long, glossy, and thick, and there in these kelp beds were all the sea otters carefully wrapped up as though they were in bed, all lying on their backs in the water with their heads sticking up and their paws together. . . . They are quite the most enchanting animals I think I have ever seen.

GERALD DURRELL

Swaying peacefully in the cold, sunlit waters of our Pacific coast are the forests of the sea. Giant kelp forms the trees of the forest while a vast array of other protists, plants, and animals dependent on the kelp complete the community. Conditions required for kelp to grow are uncommon, as the huge, fast-growing organisms require sunny, cold waters to thrive. Only in certain parts of the Pacific coast of the Americas and in limited areas off the coasts of Australia, New Zealand, and South Africa are they able to grow.

The Structure of Kelp

Anchoring itself to the rocky ocean bottom with rootlike structures known as **holdfasts** (with branches called haptera), the kelp can reach 30 meters toward the surface, sometimes growing one meter in a single day. Large, simple blades, which are leaflike in structure, gather sunlight and convert it to sugars through photosynthesis. An air bladder, or **pneumatocyst** (new MA toe sist), is filled with gases and keeps the blade afloat, maximizing its light-gathering potential. Many blades grow together at the top of the kelp and form a canopy at the water's surface. Like the canopy in a terrestrial forest, this is the most productive part of the kelp. A narrow stipe, or stemlike structure, transports nutrients from the blades in the sunny canopy to parts growing farther down in shadowed waters.

Sunlight filters through giant kelp blades in this kelp forest off the coast of California.

Kelp reproduces by alternation of generations. The kelp produces spores that settle to the bottom and grow into microscopic egg- or sperm-producing structures. The mobile sperm swims to the egg and produces a zygote, which grows into a new kelp.

Invertebrates of the Kelp Forest

Each individual kelp organism supports a large and interesting community of animals. It is along the stipe and blades and within the holdfasts that these animals find food and shelter. The kelp forest has its share of animals that feed directly on the kelp, and others that feed on these herbivores.

The top snail is a kelp eater, and the holes in the blades and stipe of the plant testify to the snail's appetite. Other animals attach themselves to the blades but do not eat the kelp. The tiny colonial bryozoan reaches tiny stinging tentacles outward to gather its prey of plankton from its stationary position on a kelp blade. Perfectly camouflaged, kelp crabs and decorator crabs scurry about on the blades and stipe, scavenging for food.

Within the holdfasts, numerous invertebrates, including brittle stars, crabs, sea stars, and worms, find shelter from predators. Some will live out their lives here, but others, like the sea stars and crabs, remain only while very young and small. They will move on when they are large enough to brave life in the kelp forest.

> 1. Why would holdfasts provide the perfect habitat for juvenile invertebrate animals?
>
> 2. How is kelp similar to a tree in a terrestrial forest? How is it different?

Other invertebrates are associated with the kelp forest because they live nearby. The octopus, considered the most intelligent of all invertebrate animals, is one of the most interesting. Capable of living in several other marine habitats, this fascinating animal frequents the rocky areas on which kelp is able to grow. Characterized by eight tentacles with responsive suckers, this mollusk has lost all but a tiny remnant of its shell and is known for its skill in camouflage. It is further classified in the class Cephalopoda, meaning "head foot"; it has undergone an evolutionary process over time known as **torsion,** in which the head and foot region have moved to the same area of the body.

The octopus explores rocky crevices with its eight arms—ready to grasp any unfortunate shrimp or crab it encounters.

The octopus has a compound eye that is very similar to the mammalian eye and allows it to see very well. This allows the animal to match its surroundings with specialized cells at the surface of its skin. The cells expand and contract to match nearby colors. Octopi also show their mood with color, flushing bright hues when angry or excited and bleaching white when frightened. They are also able to create the illusion of a sharp, bumpy skin texture when predators are near, which presumably makes them appear distasteful. Should this fail to dissuade a predator, the octopus releases a jet of dark ink, hiding its escape.

Octopi enjoy crabs, which they break open with their strong beak, but will feed on other small prey as well. Leading solitary lives in burrows dug in the sediment of soft bottoms or in rock crevices near the kelp forest and other habitats, they emerge only to hunt and mate. Mating requires cooperation between male and female as the male must insert a specialized tentacle into the **siphon** of the female. Once the sperm is deposited, the male departs, but sometimes a portion of the tentacle remains within the female's body. Fishers used to think the piece of tentacle was a parasitic worm as it was found in some animals, but not others. The female lays her fertilized eggs in a safe shelter where she can guard them and oxygenate them. She will remain with the developing young until they hatch, but she will not eat. After the young hatch and join the plankton, the female will go off by herself and die.

Fish of the Kelp Forest

Animals other than invertebrates also make their homes on the kelp plants. A keen eye can spot beautifully camouflaged animals, such as the giant kelp fish, beside a blade. Moving with the blade as it flows with the swell, this fish is nearly indistinguishable from the kelp itself and can approach kelp crabs and other small prey without being noticed. Larger fish in the forest which prey upon them are similarly tricked. Small schools of señoritas dart nervously from the shelter of the blades to grasp at small passing prey, but they quickly return. Having evolved perfect cryptic coloration, many kelp forest animals make hiding within the shadows of the canopy a way of life.

Not all kelp forest animals choose to hide, however. One of the most flamboyant and well-known is the garibaldi, a bright orange bony fish that lives along rock reefs near the kelp forest. It is seemingly unaware of divers and appears to be curious, often approaching within a meter or even centimeters. What is more likely is that the animal is anxious about its territory, which it defends for food and for its developing young, and wants to let its presence be known. Juvenile members of the species can be identified by the presence of small neon-blue spots, which are sometimes carried into adulthood. The bright colors of this inhabitant add color and richness to the forest landscape.

Several other species of fish live within the forests. The wide-mouthed cabezon, the halibut, the kelp bass, the opaleye (named for the pearly color in its eyes), the Pacific sardine, the blunt-snouted sheephead, and the tubesnout are all examples of interesting kelp forest fish.

> 3. What is the advantage of camouflage?
>
> 4. Could an animal adapted for a camouflaged life in the kelp forest survive elsewhere? Explain your answer.

Birds and Mammals of the Kelp Forest

Few birds are associated exclusively with the kelp forests, but some, like cormorants and winter loons, can be seen resting at the surface near the forest canopy and diving periodically in search of small fish to eat. Western grebes, which rise up out of the water in a courtship dance, are also found here.

Some marine mammals can be found in the kelp forest. Certain species of seal find shelter there but leave to feed in deeper waters. Gray whales traveling on their migrations sometimes enter the kelp forests. Some gather kelp into their mouths, presumably to obtain a quick meal by straining any invertebrates that might be attached, but it is unlikely they are receiving much food. Most move on soon after their brief rest in the shade and protection of the forest.

The sea otter relies on a healthy kelp forest for survival and seldom leaves. The sea otter is placed in the order Carnivora, family Mustelidae, and is closely related to the weasel. This, the smallest of all the marine mammals, lives exclusively in cold Pacific waters from the Aleutian Islands to Baja California. An estimated population of 1,500 sea otters lives off the coast of northern California, where kelp beds provide food and shelter. They spend their lives in the ocean, only venturing onto land in the rocky surf zone where they occasionally gather mussels to eat. Sea otters even sleep in the water, wrapping kelp around themselves to prevent drifting away.

Sea otters are the only marine mammals that do not insulate their bodies with blubber. They stay warm instead with a thick coat of fur that must be constantly groomed to provide the needed insulation. Any mats that develop reduce the insulating capabilities of the fur by eliminating trapped air and could be dangerous to the animal. Sea otters have a high rate of metabolism, which provides additional warmth. This means that the animal must spend nearly all of its waking hours feeding.

The sea otter feeds on a number of invertebrates including crabs, shrimps, abalone, and sea urchins. Rarely, they feed on small fish, and when food is scarce, on sea stars. The diet of the sea otter has been widely discussed and is misunderstood by many fishers who feel that the mammal competes with them for abalone.

Sea otters rest and socialize in groups called "rafts," but they forage for food alone.

In fact, it is the diet of the sea otter that helps to preserve a healthy kelp forest. Sea urchins feed on kelp, particularly on the anchoring holdfasts. The sea otter controls the sea urchins' numbers and protects the kelp. A healthy kelp forest, in turn, is necessary for the survival of abalone and other valuable shellfish.

Sea otters are one of the few species of animals known to use tools. When feeding, they float on their backs at the surface and place a flat stone or shell on their chest. They tap a newly-captured mussel or sea urchin firmly against the stone to release the edible portion of the prey. The sea otter then continually washes its food to prevent soiling its fur. The tool is placed in a flap of skin beneath the forelimb when the animal dives.

Sea otters are playful during mating and complete a chase sequence prior to the event. The female dives away from the male, and he gently pursues. Couples are quite affectionate during mating play, twisting and rolling—often moving away from the other animals into a private lagoon. This behavior may continue for several hours. Just prior to copulation, the male grasps the female by the soft tissue of the nose to hold her in place during mating. Females often bear numerous scars on the nose from this act. The females give birth to only one pup at a time and nurture their young. Males do not assist the females in the rearing process.

While hunting, females leave their pups at the surface, protected by the kelp. Upon their return, the pups greet them enthusiastically, begging for food and trying to rest on the female's upturned abdomen. Females respond by grooming and feeding their young. As the pups warm up and their fur dries, they take on a soft woolen appearance which led to them being called "woolies."

Sea otters are very curious and often do not seem to mind onlookers. They appear to be playful and fun-loving and are excellent swimmers. They are preyed upon by sharks, but for the most part have found their greatest competition from humans. Sea otters have the densest fur of any mammal. For this reason they have long been sought by fur traders. Hunted to near extinction, sea otters are now protected by law. Thought to be completely extinct in the early part of this century, a small colony was discovered in 1915, but it was kept a secret by biologists until 1938. Sea otters are especially vulnerable to oil spills, as sticky material remains on their fur and interferes with insulation. Eager to remove the strange substance from their fur, the sea otters continually groom and ingest toxic levels of oil.

Sea otters face other threats in the oceans today. There is a growing demand by restaurants for fish that are kept alive until just before cooking. The fish traps used to meet this demand also capture and drown sea otters. Groups interested in sea otter preservation are pressing for simple modifications to the traps, at negligible cost, to protect the sea otters.

Sea otters, like all marine mammals, suffer from diseases thought to be caused by unusually high levels of contaminants in their tissue. Pollution of their habitat is believed to depress immune response, which leaves them vulnerable to infection.

> 5. Why are sea otters well suited for life in the kelp forest?
>
> 6. How do sea otters protect the kelp forest that supports them?

Seasons in the Kelp Forest

Like forests on land, the kelp forest experiences changes with the seasons. In the spring and summer, when the ocean is calm and the skies sunny, the forest experiences its greatest growth. It is also in the spring that upwelling occurs, bringing cold, nutrient-rich water from the deep, fertilizing the kelp. Invertebrates and juvenile fish feed on the abundant plankton and grow quickly. Cormorants and sea otters find enough food to feed their new offspring.

Autumn is a peaceful time in the kelp forest. The luxuriant growth of summer is in full display, water is clear, and most animals are free of rearing responsibilities. This time of abundance prepares them for the difficult times ahead. In the winter when waters roughen, kelp forest dwellers must be prepared for the worst. In storm-torn winter waters, holdfasts sometimes pull away from their rocky anchors and are set adrift along with all the animals on board. Winter beaches are often littered with the remains of the huge kelp that wash ashore. Those kelp that remain attached despite the waves are tossed and tattered. Animals in the forest must weather these storms. For some this means remaining in shelters along the rock reefs nearby. Some sea otters wrap themselves in kelp to prevent being lost to the swell, while others come ashore to wait out the storms.

Threats to the Kelp-Forest Ecosystem

Humans are interested in kelp forests because the kelp provide a natural gel called algin that readily absorbs water and is used in products such as ice cream, pharmaceuticals, puddings, and toothpaste. It is also used as food for abalone in fish farms. Kelp harvesting seems to be a good example of sustainability; however, it is not well regulated and its impact on the kelp forest remains unknown. Many animals, including the sea otter, require the canopy of kelp that harvesters remove; fortunately, the entire kelp is never taken. The fast-growing nature of kelp is what makes properly-conducted harvesting tolerable.

In California, kelp has been reintroduced to the once-polluted Santa Monica Bay. The Santa Monica Baykeepers' restoration project could one day allow the kelp, fish, birds, and even sea otters that once thrived there to return.

El Niño, a warm current that moves through every few years, can devastate whole forests of kelp, which cannot tolerate temperatures much above 21°C.

> 7. How are global warming and El Niño similar? Is it possible to use the effects of El Niño as evidence of the potential dangers of global warming to marine ecosystems? Explain your answer.

CHAPTER 11 *The Open Ocean*

The greatest riches are those of the heart, and the sea is capable of literally flooding us with aesthetic and intellectual joys.

JACQUES-YVES COUSTEAU

The vast blueness of the open sea, also called the **pelagic** zone, covers 75 percent of Earth's surface. The word pelagic means "oceanic," and biologists use this term to describe any life forms that live in the open sea. Unattached, associating themselves with no substrate, pelagic organisms live drifting, swimming, or floating in the sea.

The many life forms that exist in the open ocean depend upon the presence of microscopic living things known as phytoplankton, the bottom of the food chain. Animals follow the drifting phytoplankton as they travel within oceanic currents. Only in areas where plankton grows can other animals survive.

1. Is green or blue ocean water more fertile? Explain your answer.
2. What living thing is the primary producer in open-ocean food chains?

Plankton in the Open Ocean

The word plankton means "drifter" and, whether plantlike (phytoplankton) or animal (zooplankton), these microscopic organisms are unable to break free from the flow of the ocean's currents, although most are able to propel their bodies in some way. Too small to make headway against currents, they move with them. Diatoms, dinoflagellates, foraminiferans (for a MIN i fer ans), and radiolarians are all examples of marine phytoplankton, the first two being the most common.

This microscopic view of diatoms reveals their many unusual forms.

Viewed microscopically, the ocean is teeming with life. Phytoplankton and other microbes, such as bacteria and viruses, all exist together in staggering numbers in very small volumes of water. Compounds released by one are used by another in what appears to be a highly interdependent ecosystem in a single drop of water.

Diatoms make up the majority of phytoplankton and appear in hundreds of different shapes and sizes. Glass-like silica, found in the cell walls of diatoms, gives them the look of tiny glass boxes.

Dinoflagellates, which lack the diatoms' variety of forms, have a flagellum, a whip-like tail that allows them to move. These tiny organisms, along with several other species of algae, may be responsible for a phenomenon known as "red tide." The term "red tide" describes a rapid increase in the population of dinoflagellates, whose reddish color tints the water (a population increase in algae is called an algal bloom). Simply turning the ocean water red would not necessarily merit alarm, but as most coastal residents know, fish (especially shellfish) that have been exposed to red tide should not be eaten. Dinoflagellates release a poison, which under normal circumstances appears in such minute quantities that it is not harmful to animals that ingest it. During a red tide, these dinoflagellates are eaten in enormous quantities, especially by filter feeders—invertebrates such as oysters, clams, and mussels that draw in large quantities of water and filter that which is digestible for food. This feeding technique causes the simple animals to concentrate the dinoflagellates' neurotoxin in potentially lethal concentrations. Shellfish seem to be rarely, if ever, affected by the red tide, but some are eaten by other animals. As the neurotoxin moves up the food chain it becomes more concentrated and therefore more lethal. Fortunately, areas affected by red tides can be carefully pinpointed and official closings of shellfish areas are widely heeded. Biologists know very little about what causes the dinoflagellates to bloom.

> 3. Give a definition of algal bloom.
>
> 4. Why does the dinoflagellates' neurotoxin become more concentrated in organisms higher up the food chain?

In addition to releasing 75 percent of Earth's oxygen, these phytoplankton feed all pelagic animals. Zooplankton, the drifting animal life in the open ocean, are actually a combination of many different types of animals at different stages of development. The tiny arthropods known as copepods and euphausiids (you FO zee ids), which are also called krill, the cnidarian and ctenophoran sea jellies, and the many larval forms of developing fish and invertebrates are all considered zooplankton.

Not all plankton are small: siphonophores, salps, larvaceans, and some jellies are large animal drifters. One siphonophore found in the deep ocean has been measured at 40 meters, making it the longest animal on Earth. Siphonophores are colonial animals or collections of individuals cooperating in food-gathering, movement, reproduction, and protection of the whole. Salps pump water through an internal filter to gather food, and larvaceans construct external filters for feeding and protection. Jellies drift with the current and use stinging tentacles to capture food; the largest has tentacles nearly 40 meters long.

Fish in the Open Ocean

Appearing in huge numbers as they feed on phytoplankton and one another, zooplankton feed many larger animals. Schools of fish, including anchovy and herring, feed on zooplankton and then, in turn, feed larger fish such as tuna. Still larger fish like the blue shark feed on the tuna, completing one pelagic food chain.

Schools of mackerel, bonito, marlin, and swordfish also roam the open ocean. Schooling is a very important feeding and defensive technique, especially in the open ocean. Fish living here do not have the advantages enjoyed by coastal fish that can take cover in rocks, sand, kelp, coral, or any number of other hideaways. In the open ocean, there is only the water and other fish. For protection, many fish stick together.

Using a sensitive organ called the lateral line, fish are able to detect movement among other members of the school. Such sensitivity allows schools to move as one animal and thus evade predators or pursue prey. It is theorized also that in some species, more dominant fish may be found on the interior of the school where they are best protected. Lesser members of the school are found along its fringes, the area most vulnerable to attack. Such behavior has a terrestrial equivalent; herding ungulates (hoofed mammals) structure herds in a similar manner. The "safety in numbers" concept certainly applies to fish in the open ocean.

> 5. What are the advantages of schooling?
>
> 6. In the described structure of a fish school, which members will be most likely to survive and reproduce? Of what evolutionary significance is this?

Mating in the Open Ocean

It is not only fish that school in the open ocean. Squid also form huge mating aggregations in the open sea. Males frantically search the schools for females, their heads flushing red as they approach. Once in contact with a female, the male encircles her and inserts sperm into the mantle cavity of the female with the help of a specialized tentacle. His other tentacles flush a deep red color when copulation occurs. After this ten-second mating process, the couple separates and the female lays her eggs on the ocean floor in large flower-shaped clusters called mops. A few days later, the adults die. The young hatch as miniature versions of their parents and join the other zooplankton, drifting with the currents.

Many predators, including humans, exploit these mating schools. With their normal defensive behaviors suspended as they search fervently for mates, the squid make easy prey.

> 7. What is the advantage to the squid of reproducing this way? What are the disadvantages?

Migration

Other large animal gatherings take place in quest of reproduction, and one of the most impressive is that of the salmon migration. Both Pacific and Atlantic salmon are born in freshwater rivers, which carry them to the sea where they spend their adult lives. Drawn by an ancient instinct to reproduce, the adults return to the rivers and streams in which they were born to spawn. Traveling up swift-moving rivers, the fish overcome incredible obstacles to reach the deep pools upstream where males and females who have arrived safely simultaneously release egg and sperm. Within days of spawning all die.

The mechanism that the adult salmon use to identify their home stream is still a mystery, but it is in part linked with the animals' ability to smell the stream. Unfortunately, the spawning streams and rivers are often polluted or altered in some way by humans, making them unacceptable to the salmon. But the fish will not spawn elsewhere. In addition to these pressures, it is now known that salmon cannot "smell" their stream if its pH is acidic. Acid rain caused by industrial emissions has had a devastating effect on lakes and rivers in the United States and Canada and is now affecting the life of salmon.

Salmon are also affected by logging and development along their home streams. Runoff from erosion after logging along the banks ruins some streams. In other areas, too much water is diverted for human use, leaving streams too shallow for salmon. These practices, as well as overfishing, have resulted in a worldwide decline in salmon numbers and several species are endangered.

Not all migrations in the ocean are like that of salmon, covering vast distances and drawing animals back to their place of birth from far across the sea. The midwater region, or mesopelagic zone, constitutes one quarter of the ocean. At about 200 to 1,000 meters deep, with sunlight too weak to fuel photosynthesis, there is a daily vertical migration, known as a diel migration, from the daytime depths to the surface at night. The animals that make their home in this deep and dim habitat must rely on what falls from above or migrate at night to the surface in search of food. Marine snow, or the drifting, decaying bits of protist, plant, and animal material provide food to the animals of this region. (See Chapter 12: The Abyss.)

> 8. How would you study the behavior of midwater fish?

Many species of fish migrate to gather food and reproduce. The bluefin tuna covers vast distances in a short amount of time as it travels across the Atlantic Ocean basin each year. Protective laws cover only coastal areas, leaving the bluefin tuna vulnerable to overfishing in the open sea. As understanding of fish migration expands, so must measures designed to protect dwindling populations.

Sharks in the Open Ocean

Sharks are also found in the open ocean, some in large schools and some alone. These fish have skeletons of cartilage and are members of the phylum Chordata, class Chondrichthyes. One of the keys to the shark's success is its ability to survive in various habitats, making competition for food with other sharks unnecessary. They come in a variety of sizes and shapes, with one thing in common—success in the sea.

> 9. Why is it important to avoid competition with other animals?

Sharks like this reef shark use all of their senses when locating prey. The sense of smell is especially keen.

The whale shark, the largest fish in the world, reaches lengths of 14 meters and is a harmless, toothless plankton eater. The nine-meter-long basking shark also filters plankton and small fish from the water for food. These animals, sometimes traveling in schools of up to 100 individuals, move through plankton-rich waters with mouths agape to capture their tiny prey—a posture that seems threatening, but is in fact harmless. Of the 250 species of sharks that roam the world ocean, only a few are considered in any way dangerous to humans. Large sharks include the tiger, hammerhead, blue, and great white. Only the great white ventures into cold water; most are found in temperate and tropical seas.

Sharks have a streamlined shape, allowing them to glide effortlessly through the water. Shark skin is very tough. Its scales are modified teeth known as denticles that protect the animal. Sharks' teeth are calcified and most species have many. Several rows of teeth are found in the jaw and can quickly rotate forward when teeth are lost. It is the fossilized remains of sharks' teeth that teach us that sharks have roamed the sea for 350 million years.

> 10. What information can be obtained from fossilized shark teeth?
>
> 11. Why are teeth the only shark fossil to be discovered?

All sharks lack an operculum, or gill covering. Some must therefore stay in constant motion to breathe, while others force water over the gills with muscle movement and do not have to move. Still others enter caves or other areas where freshwater seeps from the ocean floor and mixes with seawater. The high concentration of freshwater increases the oxygen content of the water and allows the animals to remain stationary. The freshwater also loosens parasites, so remoras—small fish that clean the sharks and receive leftovers in return—can more successfully remove the external pests from between the sharks' denticles. The sharks tend to be "sleepy" under such circumstances—probably lightheaded from the excess oxygen. Sharks also lack a swim bladder; the oil within the animals' large liver helps to keep them afloat.

> 12. How might oil in the shark's liver help to keep it afloat?

Other aspects of the shark's body are also noteworthy. A close look at the shark's senses shows that it has tiny pores on the underside of the rostrum (snout) called **ampullae di Lorenzini,** which are capable of detecting the tiny pulses of electricity given off by all living things. This sense allows the shark to detect the presence of potential prey even in murky water. The eyesight of the shark, once thought to be poor, is quite good, and the shark's ability to smell is well documented. A shark can detect blood in the water 400 meters away. Sharks also hear well and listen for irregular pulses that signal swimming prey. It is small wonder that the shark is such a successful predator.

All of these aspects of shark anatomy have led to many misconceptions regarding its behavior. The manner in which the animal interprets its environment is directly linked with its response to that information. Humans may be creating circumstances that lead to unusual behavior.

Great white sharks, in particular, have long been thought of as vicious, stupid beasts—bent on attacking anything in their path. This reputation arose from observations made in the wild. Drawn to the heavy scent of bait, which humans place in the water when attempting to attract sharks, the great whites have been observed lunging for and biting parts of the boat instead of large pieces of meat nearby. At first, this was interpreted as evidence of the shark's stupidity, but in fact the shark's senses may provide a better answer.

Sharks use sight as they approach within a few meters of their prey. In the closing moments, just before the strike, the animal rolls its eyes back to protect them from thrashing prey. The ampullae di Lorenzini, which detect the prey's electrical fields, are relied upon for the final strike. Metals found on boats (including the research vessels used to find the sharks) may interfere with the electrosensitive pores' ability to gather accurate information from the environment, and cause the animal to become confused. As a result, the shark may miss the prey or strike a portion of the boat nearby. Metal placed in the shark's habitat by humans is a strange and confusing substance to which the animal has had no exposure.

> 13. Why would metal in the shark's environment affect the functioning of the ampullae di Lorenzini?

Recent discoveries indicate that sharks have a variety of subtle feeding strategies. The recent increase in attacks by bull sharks may be a result of their dawn-and-dusk hunting preference. Swimmers should avoid the water in known bull-shark habitats at these times.

Other human activities may confuse the great white shark (among other species) and have led to additional misunderstandings of its behavior. From below the waves, humans on surfboards may resemble seals and sea lions (the great white shark's favorite prey) basking at the surface. Rising quickly from behind and beneath its prey, the shark strikes mid-body, then swims away to circle its wounded victim until it is weakened or dead. Humans are usually rescued before the shark returns to make a final strike, or the animal abandons the attack when it realizes that the hard fiberglass of a surfboard is not as tasty as the blubber of a seal. Again, we must seek to understand the manner in which sharks interpret their environment before we begin to draw conclusions about their behavior.

Shark Reproduction

Sharks reproduce in one of three ways, but always as the result of internally fertilizing the eggs of the female. The actual act of copulation has been rarely witnessed. As is the case with any pelagic animal, mating while floating in water presents some problems.

To keep the female still while sperm is deposited by the male, the female can expect to be either held in place by the male's sharp teeth or with structures on the male's body known as **claspers.** Biting the female behind the head, the male will hold her during mating. The skin on the back of a female's head can be up to five centimeters thicker than the male's—a necessary feature when one considers this version of shark "tenderness." Claspers are barbed structures that the male inserts into the female's genital opening ensuring they remain together until sperm is deposited.

Some sharks deposit their young in egg cases of varying shapes and sizes, which usually contain one embryo. The young develop within the protective case, nourished by a yolk sac, hatching when ready to fend for themselves. This reproductive method—depositing an egg outside the body where the young are nourished by a yolk—is called **oviparity.** For example, the horned shark lays an egg sac that protects and nourishes the embryo until hatching.

Other sharks develop within the body of the female, nourished there by a yolk sac. The young emerge as miniature versions of adult sharks, which take no interest in them after birth. This reproductive strategy is called **ovoviviparity**—young hatching from eggs within the body of the female and developing without a placenta. Often a single embryo will consume its siblings while still in utero.

Other sharks also hatch their young from eggs within their bodies, but have additional means of nourishing them. The smoothhound shark, for example, nourishes its young with a placentalike structure. This "placenta" is really a modified connection to the yolk sac and allows the embryo to receive nutrients directly from the female as well as from the yolk. This form of reproduction is known as **viviparity**—young hatching from eggs within the body of the female and receiving nourishment directly from her.

> 14. Explain the three reproductive strategies and use sharks to give an example of each.

Threats to Shark Populations

When one considers the many fascinating aspects of shark biology, known and unknown, it is clear that we should seek to understand these amazing animals and not be susceptible to irrational fears of what they may do to us. Hollywood has certainly never done sharks any favors by depicting helpless victims being eaten alive; in fact, this seldom happens. Sharks are frequently hunted for sport and in many areas far too many are taken because of the status a shark killing brings.

Sharks are in decline throughout the world because of overfishing, pollution, and the shark fin trade. Finning—removing the fins for use in shark-fin soup, then throwing the live animal back in to the sea—poses the gravest threat to shark populations today. Finning leaves sharks vulnerable to death by predators, drowning, and bleeding. Shark fin soup is a delicacy, served at important social gatherings as a symbol of wealth and prosperity. The soup, used as a thickener in chicken broth and with virtually no taste, can cost as much as $100 a bowl.

Because demand for shark fin has exploded, fishers in other, depleted commercial fisheries have begun finning in the last decade. Some countries, including Australia, Brazil, Canada, and the United States, have expressed concern over the fin trade and declining shark populations and have banned finning in their waters.

Conservation groups are targeting countries where shark fin soup is popular with education programs to increase consumer awareness. Sharks' slow reproductive cycle, compounded by intense fishing pressure, could have disastrous consequences. Commercial fishing, including finning, is not sustainable. Measures must be taken to protect these misunderstood predators. Sharks play an important role in oceanic food chains and, like all living things with which we share the earth, deserve respect.

15. What must change before fishing pressure on sharks will decline?

Rays and Skates

Rays and skates, the shark's closest relatives, are also found in the open ocean as well as in other habitats. The most striking feature of the ray is its modified pectoral fins—winglike appendages known as cephalic fins that allow it to "fly" like beautiful birds of the deep.

The manta ray is the largest of the rays, reaching widths of six meters (from wing tip to wing tip) and weights of 1,400 kilograms. This huge, gentle beast glides through the open sea feeding on plankton and small fish. The manta's curious habit of leaping out of the water may help to loosen parasites.

All rays and skates have gill slits on the ventral side of the body. Despite some of their names—sting, electric, spotted eagle—they live peacefully, gathering small shellfish, squid, fish, or plankton for food. The electric ray, as its name implies, uses jolts of electricity to stun fish that it hunts at night.

Inside this skate egg, or "mermaid's purse," are one or more developing embryos, which will emerge ready to begin life alone.

16. Why are rays classified together with sharks?

To reproduce, skates and rays mate and fertilize internally. Skates deposit an egg case containing an embryo, nourished by a yolk sac. The egg case of a skate is called a "mermaid's purse" because of its resemblance to a handbag. Rays' eggs hatch within the female's body, and rays are born fully functional.

17. Are ray and skate reproduction viviparous, ovoviviparous, or oviparous? Explain your answer.

Birds of the Open Ocean

There are several species of bird that make long migrations over the open ocean—albatrosses, petrels, and terns among them. All have some connection with this part of the ocean, and the albatross is by far the largest. There are several different species of albatross and they have the largest wing span of any bird—more than three meters. These huge, beautiful birds are so effective at gliding, they can even sleep on the wing. Gliding on steady ocean winds, they remain at sea for long periods.

Albatrosses mate for life and return to the same breeding site each year to reunite with long-separated partners. Interesting and extravagant mating displays help mates to identify each other and re-form old bonds. Raising young is difficult and the stronger the bond between partners, the easier the task.

It is the albatross's return to land that led early observers to name it the "gooney bird." The graceful flyer has difficulty landing and taking off; awkwardly trying to manage the huge wings leads to occasional stumbles and crash landings. The gathering of food for hungry chicks makes frequent landings essential.

Mating for life, despite our desire to give it a human rationale, is in fact an arrangement of convenience. Mating and raising young requires such an investment of time and energy that if finding a new mate were added to the annual ritual, the task would be insurmountable for many animals.

> 18. Why might the albatross mate for life?

Whales

Of all the open ocean's impressive inhabitants, the grandest of all are the whales. Many are found in coastal areas, while others never venture close to shore. We will consider them within the open ocean because of their swimming lifestyles. Placed in the order Cetacea, these huge mammals are further classified into two distinct suborders—Mysticeti (the baleen whales) and Odontoceti (the toothed whales). All whales have blowholes on the tops of their heads through which they breathe. Toothed whales have a single blowhole, while baleen whales have two. Family groups of whales are referred to as pods, and larger groups of many pods are called herds.

It is evident from the presence of a vestigial pelvis that all whales evolved from a terrestrial ancestor (the term vestigial refers to an organ or structure in a species that once served a function, but is no longer needed). The pelvis is used in terrestrial animals to support weight, yet whales live in the buoyant, aquatic environment of the ocean where weight is of little significance. Probably motivated to return to the sea to exploit food sources, ancient whales continued to evolve features that were supported by this lifestyle. In the water, they evolved to their huge size and became truly aquatic, having no reason to return to land.

> 19. Name a human vestigial organ.
>
> 20. Why is a pelvis an indication of terrestrial origins?

Belugas, dolphins, narwhals (NAR wals), orcas (sometimes referred to as killer whales), pilot whales, porpoises, and sperm whales are all considered toothed whales. Beaked whales, a group of very mysterious and seldom-seen animals, also are placed in the suborder Odontoceti with the toothed whales. All have teeth that allow them to pursue prey of fish, squid, and, in the case of some orcas, penguins, pinnipeds, and even other whales.

The orca lives in stable pods of up to 50 animals, maintaining constant contact with vocalizations. Each pod has its own distinctive "dialect" of clicks and whistles.

The sperm whale is the largest of the toothed whales and has the largest brain of any living thing. Males are larger than females and can reach lengths of 18 meters and weights of 45 metric tons. These animals travel the temperate seas in male-dominated pods with a wide range in age of individuals. Their teeth, for which they are classified, are found only in the lower jaw. The largest tooth recorded for a sperm whale was 28 centimeters long and weighed 1.8 kilograms.

The large head of the sperm whale makes up 30 percent of its body weight and contains spermaceti, oil thought to function in echolocation (a form of communication and navigation). The diving marvels of the cetaceans, sperm whales are able to remain underwater for up to 90 minutes and can reach depths of 2,000 meters in search of prey, such as the 18-meter-long giant squid. One can only imagine the battles in the dark depths between these two giants.

Orcas are recognizable by their distinctive black and white coloration, which serves no protective function because orcas have no natural predators. They have been called the wolves of the sea, presumably because of their cooperative hunting style. Although historically feared by humans because of their predatory ways, studies in recent years have indicated that the animals are highly intelligent and family-oriented.

Orcas exhibit two distinct lifestyle preferences. Some choose to remain in coastal waters, feeding predominantly on fish found there; these are referred to as resident orcas. Others choose to roam the open ocean, searching for much larger prey; these are referred to as transients. The resident orcas form very close family bonds and seldom, if ever, leave traditional fishing waters. Transients, on the other hand, may be rogue members of resident pods and are far more aggressive. It is the transients who feed on larger prey—penguins, seals, sea lions, and, in some cases, the great whales. The reports of orcas killing without eating animals as large as blue whales are true. Unlike the resident orcas that continually vocalize to one another, the transients move together in complete silence, perhaps to remain hidden from their mammalian prey.

Threats to Orca Populations

Humans directly compete with orcas for food in the ocean, and in rich fishing waters, clashes between the two become inevitable. Recently it was discovered that orcas pass on specific hunting strategies to their offspring. Some family groups have learned to exploit fish caught in the nets of fishers and teach their young to do the same. This has led to heated debate over the orcas' protected status under the Marine Mammal Protection Act. Environmentalists, biologists, and whale enthusiasts claim the orca has as much right to fish as humans. Fishers argue the orca has no right to plunder their nets.

In fact, it is the intense pressure placed on fish populations that has led to this confrontation. In all areas of the ocean, humans take a huge share of the sea's bounty. Marine animals that use these resources must adapt and find ways to feed themselves and their offspring. This situation is an example of just that type of adaptation, as is the recent discovery that hungry orcas are resorting to preying on sea otters in areas impoverished by human abuses (see Chapter 10, Kelp Forests).

Orcas are affected by pollution, overfishing, and excessive whale-watching boat trafffic. Other human activities have affected the health and well-being of orcas. Studies show that Puget Sound orcas have high levels of contaminants in their tissues. Among the toxic chemicals for which they were tested are polychlorinated biphenyls (PCBs), used in the United States to insulate electrical transformers and capacitors until they were banned in the 1970s. Still in use in developing countries, these toxins are slow to break down in air and water and accumulate in the fatty tissue of animals. These chemicals can weaken immune response and cause reproductive problems and skin disorders. PCBs are even passed from females' milk to offspring, which imperils the calves' developing organs and systems. Recent drops in population may be an indication that orcas are not able to cope with the degradation of their habitat.

Dolphins and Porpoises

Perhaps the best-loved of all the whales are the smallest—the dolphins and porpoises. Most species are found in temperate and tropical seas, and all prefer prey of fish and squid.

Dolphins and porpoises differ in a number of interesting ways. The larger dolphin has an elongated snout that is easy to distinguish from the blunt snout of the porpoise. Dolphins are also thought to be more intelligent than porpoises because their brains are larger in proportion to their body weight, but both are considered highly intelligent. It is the dolphin, because of its "trainability," which has become an expected presence in marine parks and aquariums.

These small whales are stunningly athletic both above and below the waves. Spinner dolphins, found in Caribbean seas, are named for their ability to leap and spin from the water. Other dolphins have been seen jumping nearly six meters from the water. Whether this jumping activity serves any function beyond pure exhilaration is not known. To see the animals at close range in the water is an experience not to be forgotten. Atlantic spotted dolphins have been known to return to the same spots in order to swim with humans.

(Belugas and narwhals are also toothed whales and will be discussed in Chapter 13, Polar Seas.)

Baleen Whales

The largest whales have no teeth, but rather fringed plates of keratin known as **baleen.** These plates catch the whales' tiny planktonic prey. It is the baleen whale that migrates to the poles to feed on plankton in the summer. This time of feeding is extremely important, as these huge animals must gain weight to make the long journey back to warm, equatorial waters to mate and bear young. They feed only rarely the rest of the year, and some not at all, so a thick supply of blubber is essential to their survival. Long summer days of feeding make this possible.

> 21. Why is it necessary for the whales to migrate to warm waters if they do not feed in these areas?

Great Whales

The blue, fin, humpback, right, and bowhead whales are called the great whales and are the largest creatures on Earth. To see such animals feed on their tiny prey is impressive. All great whales open their mouths wide and gulp in huge quantities of water and plankton. With enormous tongues, they force water out of their mouths through the baleen. Zooplankton (krill) are caught in the bristles and are then swallowed. Different whales have variations on this feeding technique.

The humpback whales, reaching lengths of 18 meters and weights of 48 metric tons, are among the most creative in their feeding. They design what is called a bubble net to catch their prey. Diving deeply, the whale releases tiny bubbles from its blowhole as it circles and rises to the surface. These bubbles trap confused krill, which will mass together in a small area to avoid the rising bubbles. The whales, together with other family members, will rise quickly through the bubble column lunging at the last moment to gather the largest mouthful of krill. Only humpbacks exhibit this technique.

Humpback whales lunge-feeding.

22. What is the advantage of building a bubble net?

Not all whales feed on the same plankton. Different-sized baleen allow only certain types of plankton to be trapped while the rest are expelled in the rush of water. In this way, whales do not compete with one another for food.

The right whale is easily identified by the rough patches of calcified skin known as callosities which appear on its head. These whales, reaching lengths of 18 meters and weights of 91 metric tons, are slow swimmers. A few summer off the coast of New England. They were named "right whales" by commercial whalers because they float after being harpooned and were easily brought aboard ship. This unfortunate characteristic led to overhunting, which significantly reduced their numbers. In an effort to save northern right whales in the Gulf of Maine, scientists have identified nearly all 350 remaining whales. Using photographs of each individual's unique fluke markings, the whales can be monitored for signs of stress or disease. A technique using a specially-designed crossbow has been devised for gathering skin samples for DNA testing.

The blue whale is the largest animal ever known to have lived on Earth, reaching lengths of 33 meters and weights of 91 metric tons. Depleted to near extinction by commercial whalers for their high yield of oil, the blue whales' population has been slow to recover despite full protection by law. Estimates of their numbers are difficult. It is believed that in 2002, blue whales number in the thousands worldwide.

> 23. Why is a pelagic population census difficult?

In addition to making it difficult for humans to count them, the blue whales' roaming lifestyle makes it difficult for them to find mates. Living alone in the huge open sea, their chances of finding a mate are slim, especially when one considers their small population. Even before they were hunted, the blue whales numbered only 100,000 worldwide, not a large population. Although fully protected by the International Whaling Commission, the blue whale is not, by any means, out of danger.

Whale Communication

All whales are known for their effective means of communicating. The toothed whales communicate by emitting sound waves from their blowholes that bounce off objects and return to them to be interpreted. These echoes tell the whales where to find prey and help them to navigate. This is called echolocation and is a form of sonar (the use of sound to detect one's surroundings). Toothed whales also convey information to one another in this way, using clicks, squeals, whistles, and moans.

Each whale may also have a signal that is like a name, a combination of clicks and squeals that is derived from that of its mother. Other individuals in the group produce the sound with their own blowholes, calling to the other family member by name.

Although biologists are certain these sounds are produced by the blowhole, there is some mystery surrounding the structures involved in amplifying the sounds when they are emitted and interpreting them when they are received. Oil contained in the structure known as the **melon** in the head of the toothed whale might amplify the sound before it leaves the whale's body. When the echoes return they are received by the whale's lower jaw, which directs the sound to the inner ear and then to the brain as a nerve impulse to be interpreted.

> 24. Why is echolocation an effective means of communicating in the sea?

Baleen whales do not echolocate, but they do use sound to communicate. All have some type of call or song that might serve several purposes. The humpback whale, for example, is called the singer of the deep. Only the male has been observed singing, so it is presumed that the song is linked with finding and keeping a mate. The songs change with the seasons; all whales in a given area pick up the variations as if they were some sort of popular tune. No humpback has been heard singing in polar feeding waters, only in breeding areas.

It is important to note that whales once lived in an ocean devoid of human sounds. Before the engines of countless ships confused and drowned out the songs and calls of whales, they could communicate over vast distances. These songs, also produced by the animals' blowhole, allowed the whales to maintain worldwide communication networks, but this is no longer possible. Southern- and Northern-Hemisphere whales have no direct contact with one another because they migrate in opposite directions. What might the songs have meant that echoed through the oceans from one end of the world to another? We will never know.

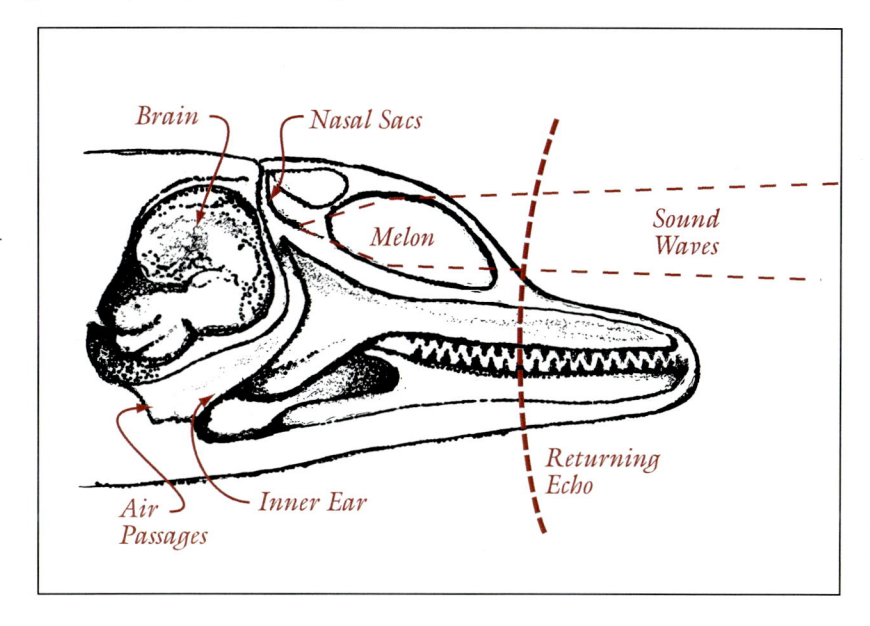

Melon tracking sound during echolocation

> 25. What advantage might whales have by keeping in contact with other whales across the globe?
>
> 26. How might losing this ability be difficult for whales?

Whales also use their bodies to communicate. Moving the tail flukes out of the water and crashing them down on the surface is called lob-tailing and may be a technique for attracting fish or concentrating krill. Orcas are known to lob-tail, as are humpbacks.

Whales are sometimes seen with their heads entirely out of the water. This behavior is known as spy-hopping, and might help them to navigate by giving them a closer look at landmarks. Both orcas and gray whales are known to spy-hop.

A distinctive body movement that is an indication of a deep dive is sounding. The caudal flukes rise out of the water fully and then disappear as the animal descends. All whales sound as they dive from the surface.

Perhaps the most interesting of all body movements is breaching. Traveling at great speeds just beneath the surface, whales are able to lunge upward, hurling their great bulk out of the water. From the smallest porpoises to the blue whale, most whales have been seen breaching. A number of different explanations exist for this behavior. Some biologists believe the whales breach to communicate with

THE OPEN OCEAN

other whales, others feel they are using the great splash to dislodge parasites, while still others point to the obvious pleasure the animals take in this aerial display. Humpbacks have been known to breach multiple times in succession—no small feat for a 45-metric-ton animal.

> 27. List the four whale body movements and give a possible explanation for each.

Threats to Whale Populations

In recent years, whales have become beloved symbols of purity and greatness in nature. Their huge size and their mysterious, gentle ways have brought international attention to their existence, which is fraught with human-induced woes. The manner in which whales have suffered from commercial whaling is well-known, and despite the fact that it is illegal, several nations still pursue these animals for commercial gain. It must be remembered that each product derived from the body of any whale has a cheaper vegetable or synthetic substitute. No "whale product" is needed to alleviate human disease or suffering.

The International Whaling Commission, the governing body for decisions regarding whales, is composed of representatives of many nations interested in whaling and conservation. Some whale populations have not improved, even under full protection; others, like the gray whale, have rebounded. Unfortunately, the gray whale was removed from the Endangered Species list in 1994; others may follow. The impact of the loss of protection remains to be seen.

> 28. Write a 100-word paragraph that supports either whaling or whale protection. In your statement, give evidence that supports your position and addresses issues advanced by opposing groups. Use clearly articulated, sensible statements to encourage your opponents to see your point. Be prepared to discuss the issue.

Threats to the Open-Ocean Ecosystem

Despite its large size, even the open ocean is widely affected by the abuses of humans. For many years, humans have used the ocean as a dumping ground. Beach closings are commonplace in some areas. Medical waste, the garbage from hospitals that is dangerous to handle, has washed ashore on beaches, causing citizens to fear the spread of disease. Obviously, such abuses have been widely practiced with the hope that the huge ocean would simply swallow up the evidence. Sewage spills are common in coastal areas and are distinct health threats. There are some sewage spills with no known cause that require beach closings.

For many years, radioactive waste from nuclear reactors was sealed in large metal drums and dropped into the open ocean. The corrosive action of saltwater caused the drums to develop leaks, and the toxic waste spread and entered the food chain. Toxic sources such as this, in combination with industrial runoff, sewage spills, pollution, and a host of other problems imperil whales and other marine mammals. The Marine Mammal Commission concluded in 1998 that pollutants are having a negative effect on all marine mammal populations.

In addition to endangering ocean inhabitants, the waste appears in fish used for human consumption. Federal testing procedures screen for such toxins, but minute quantities appear in all fish. Belugas found dead in the St. Lawrence River of New York State had unusually high levels of toxic waste in their tissues.

> 29. Why are marine mammals particularly vulnerable to contaminants?

Many types of sea vessels release sewage, plastics, food garbage, fuel waste, and other debris into the ocean. Styrofoam™ debris, found throughout the ocean, takes up to 400 years to degrade. Plastics have caused widespread damage in the ocean, as we have seen in sea turtle studies (see Chapter 7, Sandy Beaches). It is vital to avoid putting plastic bags overboard while boating or visiting the beach. Even balloons can cause injury to sea animals. Broken or deflated balloons have been found in the throats and stomachs of sick, dead, or dying animals as large as the sperm whale. Mass releases of balloons should be avoided in coastal areas. Of course, reducing the use of all disposable plastic items would be an ideal first step.

Birds, including albatrosses, have been observed bringing plastic bottle tops to their offspring to eat. The plastic will remain in the chick's stomach and will more than likely lead to the youngster's malnourishment. Like the sea turtles, the birds will have little or no room to digest foods, may feel full, and will not feed when their stomachs are full of plastics.

Nets of all kinds choke sea life. Gill nets, designed to entangle fish by their gills, are a widely-used and controversial method of capturing fish. Inexpensive drift gill nets, or drift nets, attached to the vessel and set to drift with the current, capture everything in their paths. The United Nations has banned large drift nets, some as long as 50 kilometers, and now requires that gill nets be less than 2 kilometers long.

Purse seine nets, designed to encircle large numbers of fish, are used to capture yellowfin tuna. Dolphins are sometimes captured as well. Pressure from citizens, including schoolchildren, and environmental groups forced U.S. companies to oppose the use of purse seine nets to capture tuna. Although U.S. companies will not purchase tuna captured in this way, some nations continue the practice, putting the sustainability of tuna fisheries in question. Even with measures taken to prevent the accidental catch of dolphins, tuna populations are dwindling worldwide.

Other practices imperil already depleted marine populations. Bottom dragging, also called **trawling** or dredging, uses chain-mail nets to unearth anything along the sea bottom. Each year areas twice the size of the United States are trawled. This technique, which damages bottom communities, disrupts the fish habitat, and raises sediment, is the marine equivalent of clear-cutting forests and is not sustainable.

Nearly all commercial fishing operations result in bycatch—animals captured that were not the targeted species. There is three times as much bycatch as shrimp landed by trawlers in the southeastern United States. In the Gulf of Mexico, the number climbs to five kilograms of bycatch. Bycatch accounts for some 10 percent of the total United States catch—500 million kilograms. In the Bering Sea, 16 million red king crabs were thrown away, five times the number brought to market by red crab fishers. Sharks, swordfish, and red snapper have all been depleted as bycatch.

In some areas bycatch reduction devices (BRDs) are used in a cooperative effort between fishers and scientists. Where dolphins and porpoises are accidentally caught, fishers use electronic beepers, called pingers, to warn marine mammals of the almost invisible net. Pingers have been required on gill nets in the Gulf of Maine since 1999. Turtle Exclusion Devices (TEDs), required on U.S. shrimp boats, provide trapdoors for turtles caught as bycatch by shrimp trawlers (see Chapter 7, Sandy Beaches). Birds sometimes grab at baited hooks and are captured as bycatch. To protect them, those who use longlines to capture target species reel the baited hooks underwater or fish at night.

Consumers must be aware of the impact of their decisions on fishing markets. Vote for sustainable fishing each time you buy fish in a store or restaurant. Avoid fish captured with bycatch and depleted species. Let lawmakers know you support conservation efforts. For current information, refer to Monterey Bay Aquarium's Seafood Watch (www.montereybayaquarium.org).

We must be more vigilant of the widespread damage our seemingly simple practices do to the world ocean if we are to maintain its health. The vastness of the open ocean does not protect it, so we must. The open sea, with its many mysteries, must remain healthy if we are to preserve both the interesting plants and animals found within it and the intricate life processes on which we rely.

> 30. How can individuals become better stewards of the ocean?

CHAPTER 12   *The Abyss*

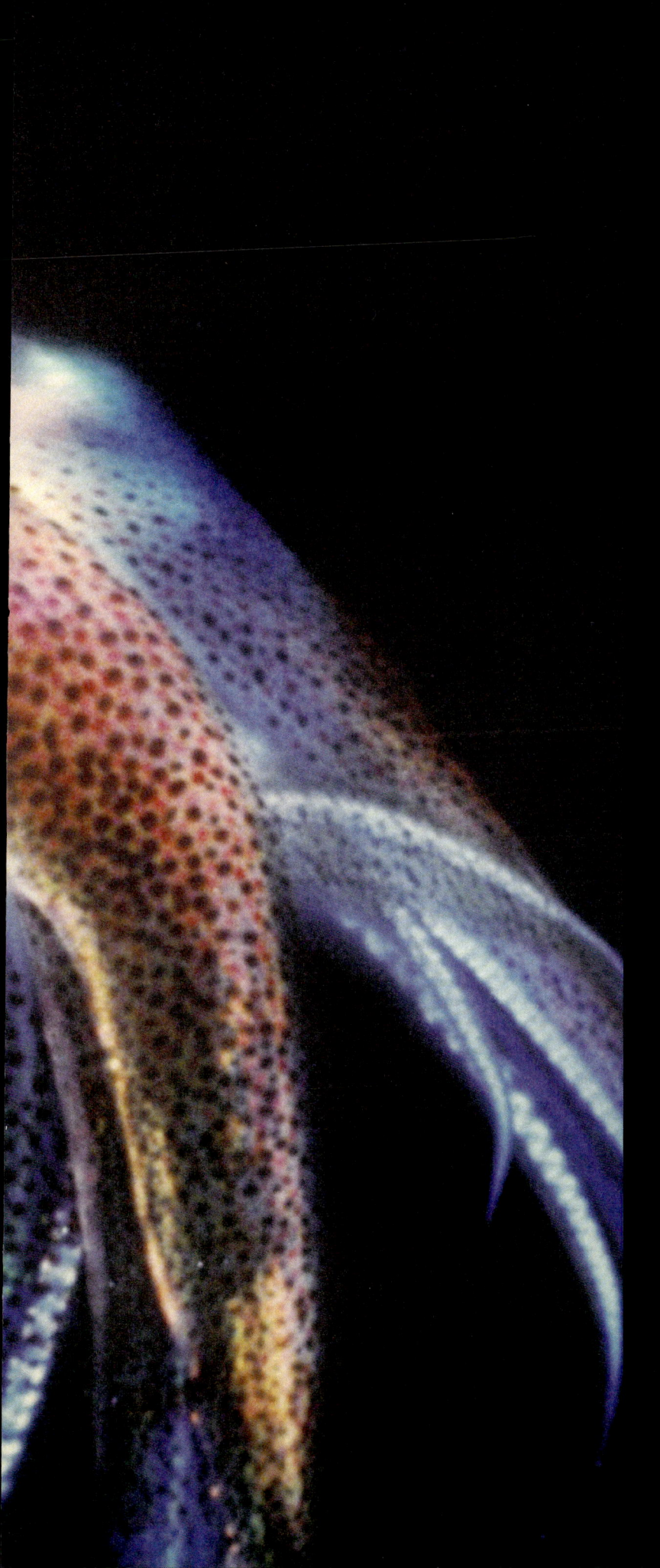

Amid the nameless sparks, unexplained luminous explosions, abortive glimpses of strange organisms . . a definite new fish or other creature.

WILLIAM BEEBE,

In the cold depths of the ocean, below the point to which sunlight penetrates, is the dark and mysterious world of the oceanic **abyss.** This habitat is the largest on Earth: one half of this planet's surface is covered by water at least 4,000 meters deep. Visible light penetrates only to a depth of 600 meters, so the **benthos,** or life of the abyss, must exist in a world of darkness. Tremendous pressure from the ocean of water above and near-freezing temperatures create living conditions unlike any other habitat on Earth.

> 1. What are the living conditions of the benthos?

Deep-Sea Exploration

Until recently, learning more of the benthos involved trawling—dragging shovel-like objects along the ocean bottom and examining whatever was unearthed. Organisms captured in this way died on the way to the surface from the rapid decrease in pressure. This technique gleaned little information about the benthos other than their basic anatomy.

Deep-sea exploration has seen exciting technological advances in recent years. In small, deep-sea submersibles, or submarines, humans have entered this underwater world, and their discoveries fire the imagination. Submersibles fall into two categories: those that carry scientists on board and remotely-operated vehicles (ROVs) that send images back from the depths. ROVs use slurp guns and pressure vessels to collect live specimens and maintain their living conditions during transport to the surface.

Life in the Abyss

Plants contain chlorophyll, which allows them to harness the sun's energy in the process known as photosynthesis. They provide food for other living things, which feed either on plants directly or on plant eaters. Plants make this energy available to all living things but need sunlight to carry out this important life process.

How then could living things exist in the ocean beneath the point where the sun penetrates, below the level at which plants can survive? In the past, biologists have theorized that the abyss must be inhabited only by scavengers, animals that feed on the drifting remains of dead sea life. If this were true, the very bottom of the ocean must be nearly lifeless, since most remains would be consumed long before reaching these depths. When scientists ventured into the abyss in their submersibles, however, this is not what they found.

A good deal of the abyss is seemingly lifeless; mile after mile of dark emptiness. But along some parts of the ocean floor, where sulphur compounds from

Earth's core spew upward from fissures known as **sea vents,** huge communities of life forms live and thrive. Chemosynthetic bacteria convert sulphur compounds to carbohydrates for use by simple animals, and thus begins the food chain. These bacteria create a food web similar to that found at the sunny surface, but without the sun. Suddenly, we have a whole new way to define life.

> 2. Why do sea-vent communities cause us to rethink what is necessary for life?
>
> 3. If life could get started with chemosynthetic organisms in the Earth's oceanic abyss, where else might it have taken hold in much the same way?

Huge species of clam, mussel, and worm, all lacking mouths and stomachs, thrive because of the presence of bacteria in their body tubes. In return for shelter, the bacteria convert sulphur compounds to digestible carbohydrates that the animals use for respiration. These bacteria also begin the food chain around cold water seeps, areas characterized by cold, mineral-rich water as rich in life as those near the hot sea vents.

Many abyssal organisms feed on the organic sediment or ooze that falls from above—the small, decaying particles of countless dead plants and animals. Along some parts of the ocean basins, animals have adaptations to avoid sinking into the thick sediment. Crabs, for example, have longer legs than their counterparts in other habitats in order to disperse their weight over a greater area.

Bioluminescence

Those animals that do not find food in the sediment have a host of creative measures to secure prey. In the darkness, the hunt-and-chase means of gathering food that is characteristic of shallower waters is impossible. Instead, patiently waiting for a chance encounter with prey or luring the unsuspecting have proven to be successful.

In the complete absence of external light many animals generate their own. In this phenomenon, known as **bioluminescence** (bio loo min ES ens), bacteria or specialized cells known as **photophores** cause the body or body part to glow. The light helps some species to lure prey, and others to identify mates. Animals and plants with a pigment known as luciferin are able

The luminous organs of the Atlantic viperfish attract prey, which the fish spears with its needlelike teeth.

to produce their own cold light, that is, light without heat. In the presence of the enzyme luciferase, luciferin and oxygen produce oxyluciferin and light, as seen in the following simplified chemical formula.

$$\text{luciferin} + \text{oxygen} \xrightarrow{\text{luciferase}} \text{oxyluciferin} + \text{light}$$

4. What must the bioluminescent lantern fish in this picture withstand as it moves to the surface each night to feed?

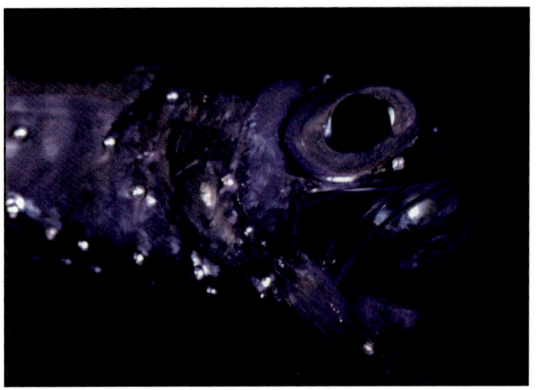

Animals of the abyss are not the only ones to use bioluminescence; at the surface some species of plankton glow when disturbed. The microscopic organisms sparkle beneath the sea when exposed to the passing fin or hand of a diver at night. No one knows why these plankton glow when disturbed.

A relative of the sea anemone known as the sea pansy glows a bright purple hue at night. This behavior may help the small, slow-moving animal to find a mate.

As in other marine habitats, fish of the abyss display remarkable adaptations for feeding and finding mates. Many use bioluminescence to assist them in some way.

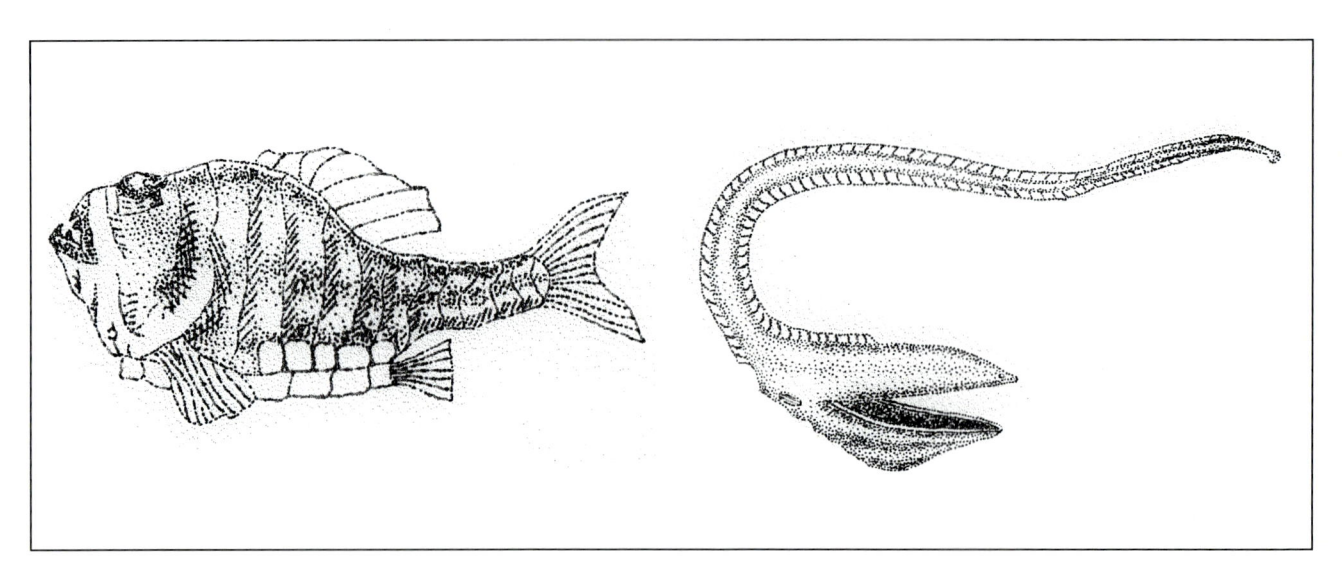

Lantern fish move to the surface to feed at night.

Left: hatchetfish
Right: pelican eel

5. How might this hatchetfish gather prey? Judging from its body design, where does it probably spend most of its time?

6. This pelican gulper eel has a glowing orb on the end of its tail. How might it be used in gathering food?

110 MARINE BIOLOGY

Left: anglerfish
Right: deep-sea shrimp

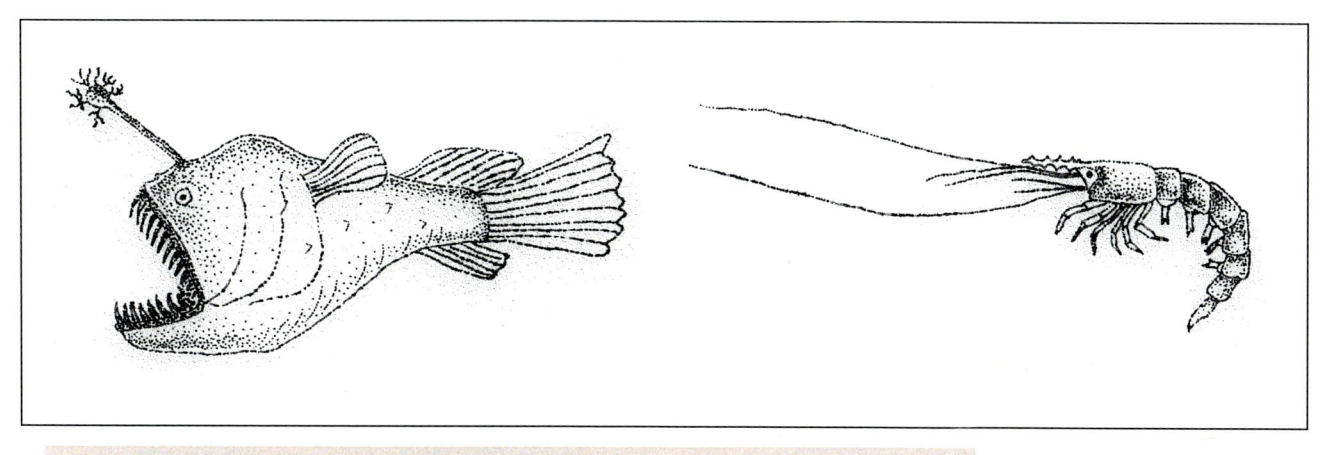

7. How might this anglerfish gather prey?

8. The deep-sea shrimp releases a cloud of light from its body when pursued. In this habitat, how would such a defense strategy succeed?

Human Impact on the Abyss

The connected nature of marine habitats suggests that toxins found in one place will appear in another. However, it is difficult to study the effects of pollution on the communities of the abyss because there is no point of comparison.

9. If you had the opportunity to do research in the abyss, what would you choose to study?

One threat to the abyss is a certainty: the development of ocean-mining technology. The deep-ocean bottom is rich in such minerals as manganese, copper, nickel, and cobalt. The minerals are contained in potato-sized nodules that could be pulled from the sea in huge numbers. Deep-water volcanic chimneys, or black smokers, some rising 50 meters from the seafloor, are often identified as potential mining sites. These towers spew rich, dark water bubbling with minerals, beneath which thrive communities like those at the sea vents. It is thought that mining operations there would produce huge quantities of sediment in the water column, blocking light and smothering communities at the ocean bottom. Sediments in the currents could remain suspended for as little as two weeks or as long as half a century. Although it is not mining there now, the United States lays claim to 73,000 square kilometers of seabed for that purpose. As other natural resources are exhausted, interest in the ocean's mineral wealth will continue.

10. What is your opinion of mining the ocean?

CHAPTER 13 *Polar Seas*

The glacier flowed over its ground as a river flows over a boulder; and since it emerged from the icy sea as from a sepulcher, it has been sorely beaten with storms; but from all those deadly, crushing, bitter experiences comes this delicate life and beauty, to teach us that what we in our faithless ignorance and fear call destruction is creation.

JOHN MUIR

Despite the forbidding nature of Earth's polar seas, they provide seasonal bounty to a vast array of marine animals. Unwelcoming in the dark of polar winter to all but a few species, these seas produce enormous blooms of plankton in the perpetual light of summer. To them are drawn many species of birds and mammals prepared to take part in the feast.

Living Conditions in the Polar Seas

The two polar areas of the world are the Arctic and the Antarctic. To the north, the Arctic is a huge mass of ice fringed by the northerly reaches of bordering continents. Beneath this ice lies the Arctic Ocean, Earth's shallowest. To the south, Antarctica is a huge land mass covered by ice that extends hundreds of miles into the sea. Polar areas are characterized by high winds, cold winters, cool summers, low precipitation, and permafrost (layers of soil that never thaw).

> 1. How do the Arctic and Antarctic differ? How are they similar?

As Earth revolves around the sun, areas at the poles are tipped fully toward the sun or fully away from it. At the equator, where sunlight strikes with its greatest strength, light and temperature are relatively consistent. At the poles, on the other hand, it's feast or famine. A summer day brings 24 hours of light and a winter day 24 hours of darkness.

Polar seas exhibit unusual and fortuitous currents known as **upwelling.** These vertical currents bring nutrients from the deep ocean to the surface where they can be utilized by plants. Such currents contribute greatly to the productivity of polar seas.

For the phytoplankton in polar waters, these long summer days and the availability of nutrients carried by upwelling currents allow them to photosynthesize unendingly, resulting in dramatic population growth. With so much to eat, the zooplankton that feed upon the phytoplankton are able to grow in number also. Larger animals come to the poles to feed on the zooplankton.

> 2. Why do phytoplankton grow so successfully in polar seas?

Krill, the small crustacean eaten by the great whales as well as by countless fish and bird species, seems to have a close connection with polar ice. Scientists have found that juvenile krill use the underside of sea ice for shelter in the winter and can be found there in great number. This fascinating crustacean is able to molt backwards, becoming less mature, and has been known to live 200 days without food.

Polar Animals

Not all animals found in polar seas have migrated there for the summer. Some spend their lives in these areas, withstanding unthinkably cold temperatures. In Antarctica, for example, the coldest temperature on Earth was recorded at –88 degrees Celsius. The seas, however, are remarkably warm compared to the land; water temperatures never fall below –2 degrees Celsius. It is the capacity of water to retain heat that keeps seas warmer than the surrounding air. Nearly all of the animals that winter in polar regions spend some or all of their time in the water.

Polar plants and animals must adapt to changes in the ice due to seasonal temperature variations. In Antarctica in March, the first month of autumn in the Southern Hemisphere, there is a great freeze, one of the most extraordinary seasonal events on Earth. Once air temperature drops to –40 degrees Celsius, the ocean starts to freeze at a rate of 5.75 kilometers per minute. By the end of winter, the Antarctic ice pack measures 47 million square kilometers.

Comb jellies, or ctenophores, move by means of eight rows of combs, or ctenes.

Fish in the Polar Seas

Polar seas do have fish populations, although the **ectothermic** (cold-blooded) nature of fish makes their presence in these areas surprising. Polar fish in both northern and southern oceans have a remarkable chemical adaptation that allows them to live in cold water. Though they would otherwise freeze solid at 4 degrees Celsius, these fish have a type of protein antifreeze in their blood.

One Antarctic species, the icefish, has no red blood cells, so its blood is as clear as water. Red blood cells contain the molecule hemoglobin, which transports oxygen. Yet the transparent blood of the icefish contains oxygen. Biologists are puzzled by the blood's ability to carry oxygen without the hemoglobin molecule. Further, the connection between the clear blood and its ability to withstand cold temperatures is not yet fully understood. Much is still to be learned about this

The cerata, or outgrowths, give this red-gilled nudibranch a delicate, lacy appearance.

phenomenon as well as the many known and unknown adaptations of these fish. Fish species in polar oceans include eelpouts, cod, snailfish, bullheads, sculpins, and flatfish.

Invertebrates in the Polar Seas

In addition to these well-adapted fish, the polar seas have surprisingly rich populations of invertebrate animals. Although there is not a large number of species, these waters support large populations of ctenophores (TEN o fours), lion's-mane jellyfish, nudibranchs (shell-less mollusks), squid, octopi, echinoderm, and planktonic crustaceans. Few species of large algae live in either polar sea; most invertebrates must feed on phytoplankton or other planktonic animal life.

3. Why do polar seas lack large algae?

4. How does the absence of large algae affect herbivorous animals?

Ice

Ice, whether completely covering the sea or merely floating within it, plays an important role in polar ecosystems. In some areas sea ice, formed from seawater, covers great expanses. In these areas the ice never completely melts. Living things that exist within the water in these areas do so beneath the ice all year long.

Both the Arctic and Antarctic have icebergs. Those in the Arctic originate from the enormous freshwater glaciers that dot the region. Glaciers that stretch to the sea from the mountains where they form are known as tidewater glaciers; they periodically calve or break off large and small portions. In the south, icebergs calve from the enormous field of ice that surrounds the Antarctic continent.

Icebergs serve as moving islands, providing safety from predators for some animals and a free ride to new feeding grounds for others.

Characteristics of different icebergs are determined by their region. Those in the Arctic are tall and jagged, reaching 150 meters above the water's surface with 85 percent of the mass lying unseen beneath the water (as the *Titanic* disaster attests). In Antarctic waters the icebergs are flat-topped and can be hundreds of kilometers across. Some of these islands of ice have reached heights of 75 meters above sea level, making them visible thousands of kilometers away. Icebergs of both the north and south provide needed resting spots to a number of marine animals.

Seals

Certain species of seals seem to be well adapted to life in cold oceans, and particularly Antarctic seas. Human hunting of seals, however, has eliminated all but ten species in Antarctica. The Ross seal, highly endangered, is the region's rarest seal. The Weddell seal, its most hardy, lives all year there, spending most of its time in the water to avoid frigid air temperatures. An accomplished diver, the Weddell seal can remain underwater for up to one hour and can reach depths of 60 meters. The ringed seal spends all year in the Arctic Ocean using the ice to conceal its movements in the winter and giving birth to its pups on ice floes in the summer.

Penguins

Penguins can be seen resting, nesting, or leaping from the water to escape aquatic predators on the huge ice floes found in southern oceans. These large, flightless birds are found only in the Southern Hemisphere and most live throughout the year in Antarctica, although one species, the Galápagos penguin, is found just south of the equator (see Chapter 3, Islands).

Penguins seem ungainly on land as they waddle about, but to see them below the waves is to witness an animal transformed. Pursuing their prey of krill, they beat their wings up and down as though flying through the water. When traveling over long distances, they move together porpoising or leaping from the water as they draw a breath. When seeking food, they move separately.

> 5. What is the advantage of traveling together over long distances?

It is only in the water that penguins can "fly." They are the only living bird that does not have hollow bones. They also store fat in the form of blubber, which gives them extra insulation from the numbing cold. Together these characteristics make for a heavy bird—one that, unlike its ancestors, cannot fly.

> 6. What in a penguin's anatomy requires it to be flightless? What in the environment allows it to be flightless?

Male and female penguins form a pair bond and then work together caring for the chicks. Most pairs nest in huge rookeries that are based on "safety in numbers." Chicks of some species are preyed upon by the large, gull-like skua, which will keep adult penguins on edge throughout the rearing process. Pairs of most species only raise one chick per year and no species raises more than two;

Penguins—like the king penguins shown here—gather into large colonies to breed, returning year after year to the same rookery.

the need to feed and protect the chick is a full-time job for both male and female.

The emperor and king penguins do not build nests of any kind. Instead they keep the egg and chick on their feet for warmth. The emperor penguins have a particularly difficult job raising offspring. These, the largest of all penguins, mate in the winter and must incubate their eggs throughout this long, dark season. Floating on a huge iceberg, the emperor penguins will take turns holding the egg and then the chick on their feet to avoid its being chilled to death. The vigilant adult goes without food during its turn to do the holding. The king penguin takes 14 months to develop and only after this investment of time will the adults allow the chick to go off on its own. Like the emperor penguin, the king penguin must also hold its chick on its feet for warmth.

7. Why would these penguin species use their feet, rather than a nest, to protect their eggs and chicks?

Walruses

Walruses, Arctic members of the order Pinnipedia, also spend time on icebergs. Highly social animals, they often try to squeeze themselves onto already crowded icebergs, but other members of the group seem to enjoy the company. They are the only members of this order that have tusks. Both males and females sport these oversized teeth, which are used in displays between males when competing for females. The ivory teeth also assist walruses in hauling their huge one-metric-ton bodies out of the water onto the ice. The tusks are also used to help the walrus unearth clams and other burrowing invertebrates that are its only food. The walrus's sensitive whiskers help it to find its prey on the soft bottoms of Arctic oceans.

Most walruses live almost exclusively on pack ice. During the coldest winter months they migrate south, but remain near ice floes.

Adult walruses have few predators, but the young are occasionally preyed upon by polar bears.

8. Name the walrus's closest relatives.

Birds and Mammals of the Polar Seas

Walruses are just one of the many species of mammal that can be found at one time or another in polar seas. In fact, these waters boast abundant bird and mammal life in the summer. Birds and mammals are **endotherms** (warm-blooded animals) and are able to withstand the cold temperatures of the polar seas. Other mammals include seals, sea lions, whales, and the polar bear. All live in or come to polar seas to exploit the rich resources available there.

Polar bears could be considered terrestrial predators, but since they receive most, if not all, of their food from the sea and are bound to life in polar oceans, we will consider them as marine. Their skill in the water is so refined that they are able to swim for three days without stopping.

Polar bears are placed in the order Carnivora, family Ursidae and are the largest carnivores on Earth, weighing half a metric ton. They feed almost exclusively on ringed seals, which they catch on the pack ice of Arctic oceans. The bears' hunting technique is impressive. Seals have breathing holes in the ice that they use to gain access to the water where they hunt for fish. The holes are well concealed with a layer of snow. Polar bears can find these holes by listening for the seal to surface. After waiting at these holes for the moment the seal appears beneath the snow, the bear attacks with powerful claws. A polar bear can behead a seal with one blow. A bear might also choose to quietly approach a seal resting on the ice. Using great stealth and effective camouflage, the polar bear sneaks up on the seal and pounces.

Male polar bears will fight over females. The males do not assist the female in the rearing of their offspring. A pregnant female bear will come inland in the winter to dig a den in a snowdrift that will shelter her. It is here in December that her blind, helpless cubs will be born in a special chamber of the den. She will have between one and four cubs, twins being the most common. She nurses them, receiving no food herself until daylight appears again to signal the end of the long, dark winter. She will then leave the den and head for the pack ice where she will be able to hunt. Having gone five months without food, she urges the still-weak cubs to make some progress toward the sea each day. She stops frequently to nurse them, digging a small nursing den each time.

The white fur of the polar bear provides camouflage against a backdrop of snow and ice.

> 9. How can the female bear survive five months without food when she is nourishing her cubs with milk?

The female bear must work quickly to teach her young how to hunt, as they will be on their own when they are two and one-half years old. The first year alone is the hardest in a polar bear's life. The young bears will have difficulty finding and catching prey with still-imperfect hunting methods and will have to avoid more aggressive males who will steal their prey. All polar bears eat the richest portion of the seal first—the skin and blubber. This is perhaps because of the constant threat from other bears who are intent on stealing another's catch.

> 10. For a polar bear, why are the skin and blubber the most important parts of the seal?

Polar bears sometimes come ashore in the summer months when rising temperatures cause much of the sea ice to melt. On land for just a few weeks, the bears mate. They also forage on the few berries and roots that can be found, but for the most part will not feed at this time. Once the temperature drops and the ice hardens, they return to the sealing grounds to begin hunting again.

Polar bears are ideally suited for polar life; warm temperatures can be hazardous to them. Because of their 11-centimeter layer of stored blubber, they can overheat if forced to exert themselves too much. If they begin to heat up, they can place themselves into a form of hibernation, slowing down their metabolic processes and cooling their bodies. Such an adaptation is essential to their survival.

Although they are not found on the ice with penguins, seals, walruses, and polar bears, there are a number of birds that travel to the poles to raise their young. Many migratory species seek the protected coasts and tundra for their summer breeding: The seasonal abundance of food and the scarcity of predators make a good combination. The polar bounty comes with a price: The short summer demands that chicks be able to travel before the cold of autumn places them in jeopardy. Adults must find mates, establish mating territories, and rear their broods in time to make the long journey back to warmer wintering grounds. A pair that has a late start will have a difficult time. Birds that summer in polar areas include several species of ducks, geese, gulls, murres, and terns.

> 11. If raising young in the Arctic or Antarctic must be timed so carefully, why don't birds choose to raise their young in the warmer wintering grounds?

The Arctic tern, a small, sleek relative of the gull, is the most amazing migratory bird of all. This bird travels from the Arctic to the Antarctic each year—40,000 kilometers round-trip. Six months of the year is required for traveling, but the remainder is spent enjoying bountiful fishing in the Arctic and Antarctic summer seas. Young are raised in the Arctic, where pairs find nesting territories on the open tundra.

Whales in the Polar Seas

Of all the animals that either live at the poles or travel to them to exploit their seasonal riches, the largest of all are the whales. Many of those species that we have considered as part of other habitats spend their summers feeding in polar seas. These include members of the suborder Mysticeti (blue, humpback, right, bowhead, and gray whales) and members of the suborder Odontoceti (belugas, orcas, narwhals, and in rare cases solitary bull sperm whales).

Some have become symbols of the pristine poles. The narwhal, the mysterious tusked whale, has a long spiraling tooth. Only males have the tusk, which can reach lengths of three meters and might be used in part to joust with other males when competing for females. Narwhals spend summers feeding on polar fish and invertebrates and are among the first to return to the polar waters in the spring. They can be seen threading their way through narrow passages in the ice, led by a dominant male who may use his tusk to help clear a path. Where they go in the winter, no one knows. They are seldom seen, so very little is known about these unicorns of the sea.

Belugas, the white whales, fill polar water with their vocalizations. These whales travel in groups of as many as 1,000 individuals. Under the Marine Mammal Protection Act, the National Marine Fisheries Service considers the beluga depleted. Only native Alaskan hunters are allowed to hunt beluga, and even they have been urged to consider taking fewer animals. Native Alaskans who hunt only for food are critical of Native commercial hunters who shoot the animals and sell the meat, displayed in local markets for $6.00 a pound.

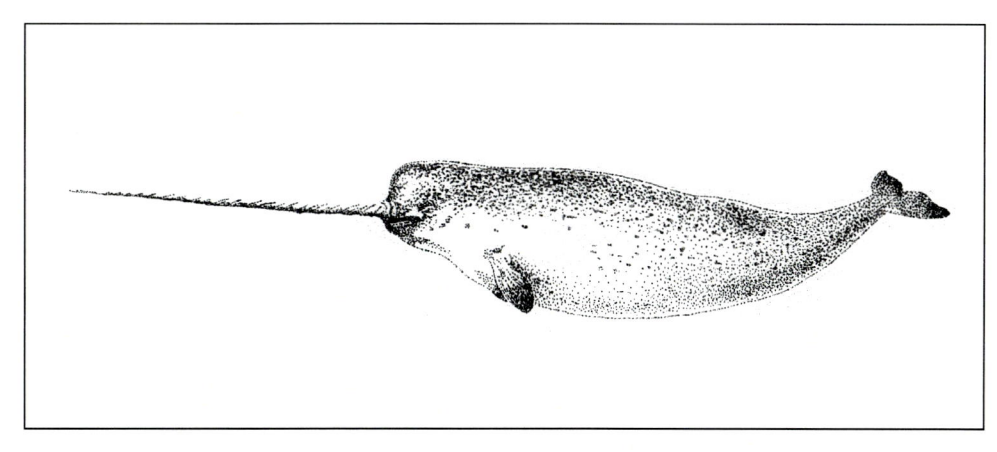

The narwhal has endured centuries of hunting pressure by poachers eager to sell the impressive tusk as a souvenir.

12. How do these air-breathing animals survive in the early-spring, ice-filled waters of the poles?

Human Impact on Polar Ecosystems

The poles, despite their seeming hardy nature, are extremely fragile. Scientists are attempting now to determine the impact of humans on this delicate system. It is not only modern practices that have left their mark on the polar seas. For hundreds of years humans have traveled to the poles to exploit the rich resources there. Despite the extremes it can withstand, the system is a simple one that is vulnerable to collapse. Overfishing and pollution are among the greatest dangers to these waters.

Perhaps the most troublesome activity in the Arctic is the oil drilling that has taken place on the North Slope in Alaska. Oil was discovered there in 1968, and the Trans-Alaska pipeline was constructed in 1977. Crossing 1,300 kilometers of sensitive tundra, the pipeline is a concern to biologists. Although built with what seemed to be great care, the design's overall durability remains to be seen.

The pipeline transports 1.8 million barrels of oil each day from Prudhoe Bay, where it is taken out of the ground, to Valdez, where it is loaded into tankers headed for points south. Tremendous danger from an oil spill is always present, both to the sensitive tundra over which the oil flows in the pipeline and to the rich waters in and around Valdez, where loaded tankers travel.

It was this danger that led environmentalists to extract specific and verifiable promises from oil interest groups in the 1970s regarding measures to contain and clean up possible spills. The public was assured that state-of-the-art equipment and highly-trained staff were available to respond at a moment's notice to an oil spill along Alaska's coast.

In March of 1989, the Exxon oil tanker *Valdez* struck a submerged rock shelf known as Bligh Reef and spilled 18 million barrels of Alaska crude oil into the waters of Prince William Sound. The slow response time of cleanup crews and questions regarding the tanker's captain enraged the public. Thousands of seabirds, sea otters, fish, and whales died. Coastlines almost equal in size to the entire Eastern Seaboard were affected. The effect this spill will have on commercial fishing interests, bird and mammal populations, and coastal zone invertebrates remains to be seen.

For animals who are directly touched by oil, the effect is deadly. A single drop of oil carried on the feather of a bird can soak through the shell of a developing chick and kill it. Birds and sea otters, desperate to clean themselves, ingest deadly quantities of oil and soon die. Attempts to clean birds and sea otters have minimal success.

Cleaning an oil spill is a difficult task. Strategies include removing the oil from the water and/or causing it to sink. Oil is lighter than water so it floats; in some cases this means it can be contained with booms and then skimmed from the water or absorbed with high-tech "sponges." If high seas are present, this system fails and crews must resort to breaking up the oil with detergents. The combination of oil, water, and detergent stirred by ocean movement forms what is known as "mousse," a slurry of toxic materials. The mousse will eventually sink or disperse and sometimes bacteria that are capable of consuming it are applied.

Most oil cleanups are considered successful when no more oil is visible, but this is a mistake. Oil is highly toxic and easily enters the food chain. Oil spills remain a great concern to polar biologists and environmentalists.

> 13. How can oil spills be handled in order to minimize damage?
>
> 14. How can individuals reduce their consumption of fossil fuels?

Naturally there is great concern over drilling in the Arctic National Wildlife Refuge. Although many studies conclude that the sensitive area should remain untouched, drilling may proceed.

Other events and issues are affecting both polar areas and the entire world. One that is particularly unsettling involves the hole in the ozone layer over Antarctica, which has been widely publicized and widely debated. Our planet is protected from the hazards of space by a narrow membrane made up of ozone molecules (three atoms of oxygen). This ozone layer prevents both excess radiation from the sun and destructive meteorites from reaching Earth's surface. Over Antarctica, a hole in this membrane the size of Europe was detected in 1972. Many studies since then are indicating the hole has formed because of the presence of CFC (chlorofluorocarbon) molecules that are released in enormous quantities by human activities.

These chemicals are either found in or are used to manufacture aerosols, air conditioning and refrigerator coolants, Styrofoam, and solvents for cleaning computer chips. One CFC molecule can destroy 100,000 molecules of ozone by removing one of the three atoms of oxygen that make up each molecule. Global wind patterns carry the pollutants to the poles where they concentrate, intensifying their dangers. Some nations have agreed to stop using CFCs, but the ozone depletion from these chemicals will continue for decades.

One of the most important questions regarding this issue is its impact on the productivity of polar phytoplankton, primary producers in all polar food chains. Exposure to excess radiation can cause a drop in phytoplankton numbers, which reduces the food available to zooplankton, including krill. The food shortage will have a devastating effect on birds and mammals of the region, including krill-eating penguins and baleen whales. Because exposure to radiation from the ozone hole will adversely affect polar plants and animals, it is important to take steps now to safeguard their food supply.

> 15. Why has the damage to the ozone layer been so significant at the poles?

As in all marine habitats, humans have made their mark on marine mammal populations. Human history in polar regions has been a story of abuse and misuse. European explorers, eager to find the elusive Northwest Passage, entered forbidding Arctic waters relying on the seemingly endless bounty to support hungry crews. Unfamiliar with humans, many polar animals were easy to kill as they had no natural fear of the human predator. Still others were slow by nature and made easy targets.

One particularly abused animal was the Steller's sea cow, the now extinct member of the order Sirenia (manatees and dugongs). Discovered in the Bering Sea in 1741, the animal was completely exterminated through overhunting by passing sea vessels within 30 years of its discovery. Very little is known of its lifestyle and only a few incomplete skeletons are known to exist. This slow and docile relative of the manatee reached lengths of ten meters and weights of several metric tons. Such size provided meat for crew members and often many more animals than could be carried on the ship were killed. The great auk, a large flightless bird, faced the same fate and is now extinct. Although measures have been taken to protect all polar species, they remain vulnerable.

> 16. Why does the fate of the Steller's sea cow represent a blow to science?

When legislation designed to protect marine mammals was developed, special considerations were made for native peoples who maintained a cultural link with the ritualized hunting of these animals. Native Americans—Alaskan Eskimos and Indians—were given the right to continue their ancestral practices or aboriginal hunting. In principle, this decision seemed sound. There is a proud history in this region of sensible hunting and use of the entire animal for sustenance, but abuses of this right have occurred in recent years.

In Antarctica, where no native humans are found, the story so far is promising. With no country claiming this continent as its own, great attention has been and continues to be given to the need for permanent protected status. The Antarctic Minerals Treaty, originally designed to protect the continent from mining forever, has been ratified by 38 nations. No mining of any kind will take place in Antarctica for the next 50 years. It is possible that large reserves of minerals, oil, and natural gas exist in Antarctica, but most nations agree that the area could not withstand the damage from such activities. Since it will be reexamined in 50 years, the treaty does not promise the permanent protection so many groups had hoped for, but Antarctica is safe for now.

Antarctica's attraction to tourists is potentially dangerous, as large numbers of visitors to sensitive breeding and feeding areas could imperil species. As elsewhere, simple activities that seem innocent can be deadly. When small planes fly over penguin rookeries to show tourists the large aggregations of birds, the loud sounds from the engines can cause the animals to stampede and many thousands of chicks and adults have been trampled. Restrictions upon "fly bys" are clearly stated, but forcing compliance is difficult.

Global warming, the gradual increase in Earth's temperature due to greenhouse gases such as carbon dioxide and methane, will change polar seas in the decades ahead. Polar ice and glaciers are melting, which will cause a steady rise in the global sea level and flooding in many coastal areas. In an ice-impoverished world, polar plants and animals will have to adapt quickly. For example, polar bears, which rely on ice floes to hunt seal, could starve.

Reducing greenhouse gases globally is a good first step toward staving off sweeping climatic changes. In 2001, the United States declined to participate in a Global Warming Treaty signed by many other nations. Despite the fact that it releases more greenhouse gases than any other nation, the United States will not be required to meet the stiff emissions criteria of participating nations.

> 17. Review the reasoning behind the U.S. government's decision not to sign the treaty. Was the decision appropriate? What will be the short- and long-term impact?

Although far away and seemingly beyond our reach, it is essential that we keep in mind the special considerations of the ocean's cold extremes—the polar seas.

CHAPTER 14 *Environmental Ethics: Approaching the Issues*

And it is a strange thing that most of the feeling we call religious, most of the mystical outcrying which is one of the most prized and used and desired reactions of our species, is really the understanding and the attempt to say that humans are related to the whole thing, related inextricably to all reality, known and unknowable. . . .

JOHN STEINBECK

The ocean is an interconnected world. For this reason, it is difficult for one habitat to be unaffected by damage to another. We must, therefore, learn to think beyond our own actions and realize the powerful effect we can, unknowingly, have on other lives and their communities. Many decisions we make, individually and collectively, have an impact on the ocean. We as a species need to be aware of that impact.

To guide our actions we must form and live by our own individual environmental ethic. To that end, some knowledge of how the issues have been addressed might be helpful.

Ethics is a moral philosophy that defines a set of principles or values of human conduct, with emphasis on determining right and wrong. Environmental ethics applies a system of values and focuses on environmental responsibility. Four basic philosophies of environmental ethics are **anthropocentrism, sentientism, biocentric individualism,** and **holism.**

Philosophies of Environmental Ethics

Anthropocentrism is the view that human interests are the most important and take precedence in all environmental matters. Regardless of the impact on other species and their habitats, the anthropocentric individual would be interested in addressing human needs first and foremost. If a species or habitat is to be protected, it is because it will be of use to humans.

> 1. Give an anthropocentric view of any issue discussed in this book.

Sentientism takes into account the needs and interests of all living things conscious of pleasure and pain. Higher animals, such as birds and mammals, would be of greatest concern to the sentientist, because plants and simple animals do not, as far as modern science now knows, experience pain or pleasure.

> 2. How does one decide which species feel pain and pleasure?
>
> 3. How would a sentientist view pollution in the estuaries?

Biocentric individualism is the view that all living things are worthy of consideration, regardless of their complexity. This view gives equal concern for both seal and sea grass; the focus is on the needs of each individual living thing.

> 4. From the perspective of biocentric individualism, how would one view the plight of the horseshoe crab?

Holism is concerned with the well-being of the community of living things, or the entire system within which they exist.

> 5. Evaluate measures that reduce the effects of global warming from a holistic point of view.
>
> 6. How can anthropocentrism be used to the advantage of individuals who represent other philosophies?

Historically, attitudes toward nature have included primarily anthropocentric views of domination and exploitation. Ingenuity, a high value on material possessions, and consumption of seemingly limitless resources have made possible unregulated use of resources.

The good news is that more and more individuals are adopting a more holistic environmental ethic and support the idea that humans are not the only valuable living thing. Nature does not exist for human use alone; other species have the right to live and thrive without human interference. Stewardship of resources is imperative if future generations are to succeed.

Sustainability requires commitment to meeting current needs without exhausting resources or compromising the future. This concept, expressed in development, politics, and individual action in a community, is crucial to any approach to marine environmental issues. By raising consciousness about the importance of balance in humanity's relationship to nature, we are reaching for the ideal of sustainability. Having this ideal as part of our own environmental ethic is imperative to the future of the species. The planet has an astounding capacity for adjustment, cleansing, and renewal. If we commit ourselves to sustainable lifestyles, the future brightens for all. This idea is not new.

In our every deliberation, we must consider the impact of our decisions on the next seven generations.
                    from the Great Law of the Iroquois Confederacy

> 7. Discuss the concept of sustainability in relation to one of the marine habitats discussed in this book.
>
> 8. How do you address most environmental issues? Might you take a different approach depending upon the issue?

You share this water planet with a beautiful array of other life forms—coexisting in an unthinkably complex and interesting living system. Make a point, in whatever you choose to do in life, to be a constructive component of that system, living with gratitude, respect, and reverence for all that surrounds you.

> *The main ingredients of an environmental ethic are caring about the planet and all of its inhabitants, allowing unselfishness to control the immediate self-interest that harms others, and living each day so as to leave the lightest possible footprints on the planet.*
>
> Robert Cahn

Glossary

abyss—region of the ocean basin that lies below the continental slope

ampullae di Lorenzini—pores on the heads of sharks that are sensitive to electrical fields

Annelida—Members of this phylum are segmented worms; includes polychaetes

anthropocentrism—a point of view that regards humans as central and superior in any system

Arthropoda—Animals in this phylum share two characteristics: bodies encased in an exoskeleton and jointed appendages; includes crustaceans

atoll—a coral island and its reef nearly or completely enclosing a lagoon

baleen—a series of fringed plates in the mouths of Mysticeti whales that strain krill and small fish from the water

benthos—animals that inhabit the sea bottom

biocentric individualism—the view that all living things are worthy regardless of their complexity

bioluminescence—(bio loo min ES ens) light produced by living things

blade—the leaflike structure on a plantlike organism such as kelp

calyx—(KA lix) the cup-shaped stony structure that houses the coral polyp; many calyxes together form a coral colony

Chondrichthyes—(con DRIK theez) the class of animals in the phylum Chordata that have cartilaginous skeletons; includes sharks and rays

chromatophores—(crow MA toe fours) pigment cells usually found in the skin that can contract or expand to alter color

claspers—structures on the male shark that prevent the female from moving during copulation

Cnidaria—(ni DARE ee ah) the phylum of animals characterized by stinging cells known as nematocysts; includes anemones, jellyfish, corals, and hydroids

commensalism—a symbiotic relationship between organisms of different species in which one benefits and the other neither benefits nor suffers

continental rise—a leveling of the dramatic drop along the continental slope

continental shelf—the portion of the seafloor that extends from the low-tide mark to the continental slope

continental slope—the steep slope that extends from the continental shelf seaward to the abyss

coralline algae—protists whose hard, stony bodies resemble coral

crustaceans—members of the subphyla Crustacea including lobster, shrimp, copepods, and barnacles; some have calcium carbonate in their hard exoskeletons

cryptic coloration—coloration that camouflages an animal within its surroundings

detritus—(de TRY tus) decayed plant and animal material

diatoms—(DIE a toms) microscopic protists that make up the majority of marine phytoplankton

dinoflagellates—phytoplankton responsible for red tides

dorsal—pertaining to or situated in or near the back

El Niño—a warm current that periodically enters ordinarily cold-water seas

ectothermic—cold-blooded

endotherms—warm-blooded animals

epifauna—animals living above the sediment in the subtidal soft bottoms

estuary—(ES choo air ee) a partially enclosed body of water with free access to the open ocean, where seawater and freshwater mix and where the tides affect water movement

Gastropoda—the class of animals in the phylum Mollusca that are characterized by spiraling shells

global warming—temperatures rise at Earth's surface as gases from human activites such as carbon dioxide and methane accumulate in the atmosphere and trap heat

groins—hard structures built perpendicular to the beach in attempts to trap sand moving offshore and avoid erosion

guyots—(gee O) submerged mountains that have flattened tops

holdfasts—rootlike structures found on plantlike organisms such as kelp

holism—a view that places primary emphasis on the well-being of an entire system of living things

imprinting—to fix firmly in the mind either through smell or some other mechanism the location of a home stream or beach (as is seen in salmon and sea turtles)

infauna—animals living in the sediment of subtidal soft bottoms

invertebrate—any animal lacking a backbone

jetties—hard structures built next to inlets to prevent sand from moving in and closing them

keratin—a protein found in certain tissues, such as the baleen of whales

mantle—the fleshy fold of tissue in mollusks that secretes a fluid that becomes the shell

melon—a structure found in the heads of echolocating Odontoceti whales that may allow them to interpret returning sound waves

Mollusca—the phylum of animals that are characterized by a nonsegmented muscular foot enclosed in a mantle or shell; includes scallops, oysters, gastropods, squid, and octopi

mucus—a slimy substance secreted by the mucous membranes

mutualism—a symbiotic relationship between organisms of different species in which both benefit

nematocysts—stinging cells, characteristic of members of the phylum Cnidaria, which function in protection and gathering prey

nudibranchs—(NUDE i branks) brightly-colored members of the phylum Mollusca that lack a shell

oviparity—a form of reproduction that involves laying eggs that develop outside the body of the female; typical of some species of shark and of all birds

ovoviviparity—a form of reproduction that involves the formation of eggs that hatch inside the body of the female and the emergence of well-formed, independent individuals; young receive no nourishment from the mother other than that provided by the egg yolk while inside her body; characteristic of some species of shark

parapodia—paddlelike appendages, found on members of the phylum Annelida, which aid movement

parasitism—a symbiotic relationship between organisms of different species in which one is harmed and the other benefits

pectoral—pertaining to or located in or near the chest

pelagic—relating to the ocean far from land

photophores—cells in some animals that produce light

plankton—small protists, plants, and animals that float in the ocean, unable to break free from the flow of currents; includes phytoplankton and zooplankton

plate tectonics—the study of Earth's crustal plates and the forces that cause them to drift

pneumatocyst—(new MA toe sist) the air bladder on the blade of kelp that helps keep the leaflike structure afloat

pod—a group of whales consisting of related members, typically a family

polychaete—(POL i keets) marine segmented worm

polyp—the body form of cnidarians that remains attached to some substrate

Porifera—the simplest phylum of animals, characterized by pores through which food is filtered; includes the sponges

seamounts—submerged mountains

sea vents—fissures in the seafloor from which compounds pour, supporting communities of abyssal organisms

seawalls—hard structures built parallel to beaches, intended to prevent sand erosion

sentientism—a point of view that places the needs of organisms that feel pleasure and pain above all else

setae—(SE tee) small, fingerlike projections attached to parapodia on members of the phylum Annelida, which aid in movement

siphon—a tubelike structure in members of the phylum Mollusca that draws in or expels fluids

spicules—the latticelike skeletal structures of members of the phylum Porifera (sponges) that supports the animal; formed from spongin, silica, or calcium carbonate

substrata—the substances in which organisms take root or attach; include mud, sand, rock, and coral

symbiosis—a relationship between members of different species that is advantageous to one or both species

torsion—the evolutionary twisting of members of the class Cephalopoda (squid, octopi, nautilus) that resulted in the head and feet of these mollusks developing in the same area of the body

trawling—a fishing or sampling method that involves dragging a net along the sea bottom in order to capture marine life

tsunami—(su NAH mee) a seismic wave generated by a sudden movement of the sea floor

upwelling—the movement of water from any depth toward the surface

viviparity—a reproductive method that involves the formation of eggs that hatch inside the body of the female; Young receive some form of nourishment from both the egg and from a modified egg tube; characteristic of some species of shark

zooxanthellae—(zo zan THEL ee) symbiotic algae that live in the tissues of corals and other animals, giving nourishment through photosynthesis to their hosts and receiving shelter in return

For Further Reading

Brower, Kenneth. *Realms of the Sea.* Washington, DC: National Geographic Society, 1991.

Carson, Rachel. *The Edge of the Sea.* Boston: Houghton Mifflin Company, 1955.

Carson, Rachel. *Under the Sea Wind.* New York: Truman Talley Books/Plume, 1941.

Coleman, Neville. *Encyclopedia of Marine Animals.* New York: Angus & Robertson, 1991.

Cousteau, Jacques. *The Ocean World.* New York: Harry N. Abrams, Inc., 1979.

Cousteau, Jacques. *Whales.* New York: Harry N. Abrams, Inc., 1986.

Davidson, Osha Gray. *The Enchanted Braid: Coming to Terms with Nature on the Coral Reef.* New York: John Wiley and Sons Inc., 1998.

Earle, Sylvia. *Sea Change: A Message of the Oceans.* New York: Fawcett Books, 1996.

Gray, William. *Coral Reefs and Islands: The Natural History of a Threatened Paradise.* Rydalmere, New South Wales, AUS: Hodder & Stoughton, 1993.

Helvarg, David. *Blue Frontier: Saving America's Living Seas.* New York: W.H. Freeman & Co, 2001

Lopez, Barry. *Arctic Dreams.* New York: Bantam Books, 1989.

MacInnis, Joseph. *Saving the Oceans.* Toronto: Key Porter Books, 1992.

Newbert, Christopher. *Within a Rainbowed Sea.* Honolulu: Beyond Words Publishing Company, 1981.

Seaborn, Charles. *Underwater Wilderness: Life in America's National Marine Sanctuaries and Reserves.* Niwot, CO: Roberts Rinehart, Publisher, 1996.

Snyderman, Marty, with The International Oceanographic Foundation. *Ocean Life: Discovering the World Beneath the Seas.* Lincolnwood, IL: Publications International, Ltd., 1991.

Photo Credits

Courtesy of Photo Researchers, Inc.
    Jean Marie Bussot—p. 109
    François Gohier—p. 96
    Dan Guravich—p. 34
    Robert Hermes—p. 115 (top)
    Paolo Koch—p. 59 (bottom)
    Stephen J. Krasemann—p. 26, p. 28
    Neil McDaniel—p. 62
    D. P. Wilson/Science Source—p. 86
    Dr. Paul A. Zahl—p. 110

Bob Cranston/Jeff Rotman Photo—p. 90

Becky Fernald—p. 70

Amy Sauter Hill—p. 11 (top), p. 33, p. 36, p. 37, p. 43, p. 55, p. 56, p. 59 (top), p. 64 (top), p. 64 (middle), p. 66, p. 67, p. 71, p. 72, p. 73 (top), p. 73 (middle), p. 73 (bottom), p. 75

Jeff Rotman—p. 5, p. 10, p. 12, p. 13, p. 17, p. 32, pp. 46–47, p. 50, p. 63 (top), p. 64 (bottom), p. 78

Index

A

abyss, oceanic
  human impact on, 111–112
  life in, 108–110
acid rain, 89
albatrosses, 95, 103
algae, 33, 86
  beneficial aspects of, 18
  coralline, 10, 71
  farming of, by owl limpets, 63
  harm to coral reefs caused by brown, 20
  mats of, 14
  red, 71
  in tide pools, 71
  zooxanthellae, 11
algal bloom, 86. *See also* algae
ampullae di Lorenzini, 91–92. *See also* sharks
anemones, 62, 71, 74
Annelida, 12, 49
Antarctic, 114, 115, 116, 117, 121
Antarctica, 114, 115, 117, 124–125
  depletion of ozone layer over, 123
Antarctic Minerals Treaty, 124
anthropocentrism, 128, 129
Arctic, 114, 116, 118, 121
Arctic National Wildlife Refuge, 123
Arctic Ocean, 114, 117
Arctic tern, 120–121
Arthropoda, 34, 40, 73
arthropods, 64, 73, 74, 87
atolls, 10, 25. *See also* coral reefs
Australian Plate, 27

B

bacteria, 32, 86
  chemosynthetic, 109
baleen, 98. *See also* whales, baleen
bays, 40–45
beaches, sandy
  bird species found along, 57–58
  formation of, 54
  importance of dunes to, 59
  mammals found on, 58
  protecting, 59
  reproduction on, 55–57
  of the United States, 54
Beagle, HMS, expedition of, 26
benthos, 108
biocentric individualism, 128
bioluminescence, 109–110
birds
  of estuaries, 35–36
  on Galápagos Islands, 25
  of kelp forest, 80
  of open ocean, 95
  of polar seas, 120–121
  of rocky shores, 65–66
  varying body designs of, 35–36
bivalves, 34
Bonaire, 27
breaching, 101–102. *See also* whales
brittle stars, 74, 79
bryozoans, 78
bycatch reduction devices (BRDs), 104. *See also* fishers

C

callosities, 99
calyxes, 10, 12, 14
Caribbean Plate, 27
Catalina Island Conservancy, 29
Channel Islands, 26
Chesapeake Bay, 32
chlorofluorocarbons (CFCs), 123
chlorophyll, 108
Chondrichthyes, 50
chromatophores, 50
cilia, 48
Cnidaria, 10, 71
coloration
  to advertise presence, 13–14, 80
  as camouflage, 13, 18, 41, 50, 79
  cryptic, 13, 18, 80
commensalism, 17. *See also* symbiosis
continental rise, 6
continental shelf, 6, 28, 54
continental slope, 6
coral, 10. *See also* coral reefs
  bleaching, 20–21
  predators of, 12–13
  reproduction, 13
  unregulated harvesting of, 20
coral reefs. *See also* coral
  building of, 10–11
  compared to rain forests, 19
  fish on, 13–16
  Hawaiian, 19, 24–25
  invertebrates living on, 11
  symbiosis on, 16–19
  threats to, 19–21
Coriolis force, 3
crabs, 64, 79, 109
Crustacea, 73
crustaceans, 15
ctenophores, 116
currents, 3–4, 86
  temperature variations of, 4
  vertical, of polar seas, 114. *See also* polar seas

D

Darwin, Charles, 25–26
DDT, negative impact of, 35
detritus, 32, 33, 34, 48
development
  disruption to tide-pool areas by, 75
  negative impact of, 28, 29, 36, 45, 59
diatoms, 48, 86
dinoflagellates, 86–87
dolphins, 25, 96, 98, 104
  "beaching" of, 58
dredging, disturbance caused by, 36–37
dugongs, 36, 43

E

Earth
  composition of, 6–7
  largest habitat on, 108
  violent beginnings of, 2
earthquakes, 27
Echinodermata, 12–13, 18, 62–63
echinoderms, success in tide pools of, 74
echolocation, 96, 100. *See also* whales

ecosystems
    fragility of Galápagos Islands, 26
    human activities helpful to coastal, 45
    human impact on polar, 122–125
    minimizing tourist impact on, 27
    role of ice in polar, 116–117
    threats to, 28, 36–37, 59, 67, 75, 83, 102–105
    tide-pool, 70–75
ectotherms, 115
El Niño, 4, 83
Endangered Species list, 102
endotherms, 119
environmental ethics, 128–130
epifauna, 48, 50
erosion, 28, 54, 59, 89
estuaries
    birds of, 35–36
    destruction of, 36
    formation of, 32
    invertebrates in, 33–34
    plants of, 32–33
    seasonal species of, 34–35
    threats to ecosystems of, 36–37
evolution, 2, 25
exploration, deep-sea, 108
Exxon *Valdez* oil spill, 122

F
Federal Marine Mammal Protection Act of 1972, 67
fish, 41
    on coral reefs, 13–16
    ectothermic nature of, 115
    juvenile, found in estuaries, 35
    of kelp forest, 80
    migration, 90
    near Galápagos Islands, 25
    nest-building behaviors of, 15–16
    in open ocean, 87–88
    in polar seas, 115–116
    in tide pools, 75
fishers
    eel, 40–41
    finning of sharks by, 93–94
    harmful practices of, 19–20
    illegal activities by, 41
    nets of, 103–104
    overfishing by, 26, 45, 124
    pinnipeds viewed as competition by, 67
    relationship of orcas and, 97
    threats to sea turtles by, 57
    tuna, 103
Florida Keys, 25
Florida Keys National Marine Sanctuary, 19
foraminiferans, 86
Fundy, Bay of, 5
fungi, 32

G
Galápagos Islands, 25–26
    tortoises, 29
Gastropoda, 12
gastropods, 63
giant squid, 96
glaciers, 116
global warming, 20, 125
Global Warming Treaty, 125
gonozooids, 72
Great Barrier Reef, 10
greenhouse gases, 125
groins, 28
Gulf of California, creation of, 27
Gulf Stream, 4, 27
guyots, 6
gyres, 3–4. *See also* currents

H
habitats, 3
    destruction of sea horse, 41
    intertidal, 4
    manatee, encroachment, 43
    rocky, 64. *See also* shores, rocky
    sponges as, 11
    subtidal soft-bottom, 48–50
hard stabilization, 28, 59
Hawaiian Islands, 19, 24–25, 29
hermaphrodites, 73
hermit crabs, 73
holdfasts, 78, 79, 83
holism, 131
horseshoe crabs, 40–41

I
ice, 116–117
ice age, last, 26–27, 28
icebergs, 116–117, 118
icefish, 115–116
imprinting, 56
infauna, 48
inland waterways, 40–45
International Whaling Commission, 100, 102
invertebrates
    on coral reefs, 11
    in estuaries, 33–34
    filter feeders, 87
    of kelp forest, 78–80
    in polar seas, 116
    on rocky shores, 62–65
    of sandy beaches, 54
    sponges, as habitats for, 11
    of subtidal soft bottoms, 48–50
    in tide pools, 71–74
islands. *See also* Galápagos Islands; Hawaiian Islands
    barrier, 28–29
    Caribbean, 27–28
    continental, 26–27
    formation of, 24–25
    negative impact of human activities on, 28–29

J
jetties, 28

K
kelp. *See also* kelp forests
    blades, 71, 78, 80
    harvesting, 83
    structure of, 78
kelp forests
    birds of, 80
    fish of, 80
    invertebrates of, 78–80
    mammals of, 81–82
    seasons in, 83
keratin, 10
krill, 99, 101, 116, 123. *See also* zooplankton
    connection with polar ice of, 114

L
lagoons, 24, 40–45
Laysan Island, 25
limpets, 63, 72
    owl, 63–64
lionfish, 13–14
lob-tailing, 101. *See also* whales
luciferin, 109–110

M
mammals
    found on sandy beaches, 58
    of kelp forest, 81–82

marine, 81
  of polar seas, 119–120
  of rocky shores, 66–67
manatees, 36, 42–44
mangroves, 25, 33
mangrove swamps, 33
Marianas Trench, 6
Marine Mammal Commission, 103
Marine Mammal Protection Act, 97, 121
marshes, 33
Mauna Kea, 24
medusas, 72
mesopelagic zone, 89
migration, 44
  bird, 95, 120–121
  diel, 89
  fish, 89
Mollusca, 12, 34, 62, 63, 72
mollusks, 72–73, 79
Monterey Bay Aquarium, 104
moray eel, 15
mudflats, 33–34, 54, 57
mussels, 62, 63, 72
mutualism, 17. *See also* symbiosis

N

narwhals, 96, 121. *See also* whales
National Estuarine Research Reserve System, 36
National Marine Fisheries Service, 121
natural selection, 3, 24
nematocysts, 10
Nematoda, 34
New Zealand, 27
North Slope, Alaska, oil discovery, 122
nudibranchs, 12, 73

O

ocean(s). *See also* abyss, oceanic
  ancient, 2
  as dumping ground, 102–103
  effect of temperature on, 4
  freezing point of, 115
  microscopic life of, 86
  -mining technology, 111–112
  open
    birds of, 95
    fish in, 87–88
    mating in, 88
    plankton in, 86–87
    sharks in, 90–92
  pressure, 5–6
  salinity of, 2. *See also* salinity
  tides, 5. *See also* tides
octopus, 79–80
oil spills, 75
  Exxon *Valdez,* 122
  surrounding Galápagos Islands, 26
orcas, 58, 96–97, 121. *See also* whales
  threats to, 97–98
organisms
  abyssal, adaptations of, 109
  environment of, 3
  pelagic, 86
Outer Banks, North Carolina, 28
oviparity, 93
ovoviviparity, 93
ozone layer, hole in, 123

P

Pacific Plate, 27
parapodia, 49
parasitism, 17. *See also* symbiosis
parrotfish, 14
pelagic zone, 86. *See also* ocean(s), open
penguins
  on Galápagos Islands, 25, 117
  incubation of eggs by, 118
  rookeries of, 117–118
    negative effect of tourism on, 125
Peru Current, 25
pH, 70, 89
photophores, 109
photosynthesis, 11, 32, 48, 70, 114
phytoplankton, 86, 114
pingers, 104
pinnipeds, 58, 66–67
Pinta Island tortoise, 26
plankton, 18, 74, 86, 87, 99
  that glow when disturbed, 110. *See also* bioluminesence
plants
  in estuaries, 32–33
  need of sunlight by, 108. *See also* photosynthesis
pneumatocyst, 78
pods, whale, 58, 95, 96, 97. *See also* whales
polar bears, 119–120
polar seas
  animals of, 115
  birds of, 120–121
  fish in, 115–116
  invertebrates in, 116
  living conditions in, 114
  mammals of, 119–120
  whales in, 121
pollutants, 37, 43, 45, 89, 102–103
pollution, 82, 97, 102–103, 122
polychaetes, 49–50
  in rocky habitats, 64
polychlorinated biphenyls (PCBs), 97–98
polyps, 10, 12, 14, 20, 72
porcupine fish, 15
Porifera, 11. *See also* sponges
porpoises, 98, 101, 104
pressure, 5–6
protists, 32, 48, 70, 78. *See also* kelp
puffins, 66

R

radiolarians, 86
rays, 50, 94
red tide, 86–87
remotely operated vehicles (ROVs), 108
reptiles, marine, 25, 42, 65
rockfish, 14

S

salinity
  changes
    in intertidal zone, 70
    mammals tolerant of, 36
    manatee tolerance to, 42
  on coral reefs, 13
  fluctuations of estuary, 32
  of ocean, 2
salmon, 89
salt marshes, 33. *See also* estuaries
sand, formation of, 28
Santa Cruz Island, California, 26
Santa Monica Baykeepers' restoration project, 83
schooling, 88. *See also* fish
seafloor, 6–7
sea grass, 33
  communities, 34
  stability provided by, 40
sea hares, 72–73
sea horses, 41
sea lions, 25, 66–67
  differences between seals and, 67

seals, 66–67
   of polar seas, 117
seamounts, 6
sea otters, 81, 83
   mating of, 82
   use of tools by, 81–82
sea snakes, 42
sea squirts, 64–65
sea stars, 74, 79
   crown-of-thorns, 12–13
   as predators, 62–63
sea turtles, 25, 42, 55–57
sea urchins, 15, 20, 74
sea vents, 109
seawalls, 28
sentientism, 128
setae, 49
shark fin soup, 93–94
sharks, 82
   anatomy of, 90–91
   feeding strategies of, 92
   great white, 66, 91
   in the open ocean, 90–92
   relatives of, 50, 94. *See also* rays; skates
   reproduction of, 92–93
   threats to, 93–94
shores, rocky
   birds of, 65–66
   invertebrates on, 62–65
   mammals of, 66–67
   reptiles of, 65
Sirenia, 36, 43
skates, 50, 94
snails, 12, 63, 78
sounding, 101. *See also* whales
Spartina grasses, 33
species
   adaptability of, 2–3, 6
   cooperative relationships among, 19
   endangered, 25
   evolution of island, 24
   extinction of, 26, 124
   fish, within kelp forests, 80
   on Galápagos Islands, 25
   seasonal, of estuaries, 35
spermaceti, 96
spicules, 11
sponges, 11, 18
spongeweed, 71
spy-hopping, 101. *See also* whales

Steller sea lion, 67
Steller's sea cow, 43, 124
stewardship, 29, 104–105, 129
stipes, 78
subduction, 7
substrata, 32
subtidal soft bottoms
   invertebrates of, 48–50
   vertebrates of, 50
sustainability, 104, 129
symbiosis, 16–19

T

tectonic plates, 7, 24, 27, 28
tectonics, plate, 6
temperature, 4
   in Antarctica, 115
   of Caribbean waters, 27
   changes in intertidal zone, 70
   effect on coral of increase in, 20, 21
   effect on kelp of, 83
   for reef-building corals, 11
tide pools, 4
   algae in, 71
   fish in, 75
   invertebrates in, 71–74
   living conditions in, 70–75
   organisms in, 71
tides, 5, 63, 70
Titanic disaster, 116
torsion, 79
Trans-Alaska pipeline, concern about, 124
trawling, 41, 104, 108
triggerfish, 15, 16
tsunami, 4
Turtle Exclusion Devices (TEDs), 57, 104

U

ungulates, 88
United Nations, banning of large drift nets by, 103–104
upwelling, 114. *See also* currents

V

Vertebrata, 64
viruses, 86
viviparity, 93
volcanoes, 24, 27

W

walruses, 118
waste
   in intertidal zone, 70
   organic, 19
   toxic, 103
water, 2. *See also* ocean(s)
   ecosystem in drop of ocean, 86
   heat-retention capacity of, 115
waves, 4, 5, 54, 70
   structures designed to reduce action of, 28
wetlands, coastal. *See* estuaries
whales, 95–102
   baleen, 95, 98, 100, 123
   "beaching" of, 58–59
   beaked, 96
   beluga, 96, 103, 121
   blue, 99–100, 101, 121
   communication of, 100–102, 121
   distinctive movement of, 101–102
   gray, 44–45, 81, 121
   great, 98–100
   humpback, 44, 100–101, 102, 121
   near Galápagos Islands, 25
   in polar seas, 121
   right, 99
   sperm, 25, 96, 121
   threats to, 102
   toothed, 95, 96, 100
World Trade Organization, 57
worms, marine, 48–50, 72, 79. *See also* polychaetes
wrasse, 16
   cleaner, 17
   humphead, depletion of, 20

Z

zooplankton, 41, 86, 87, 99, 114
zooxanthellae, 11, 18, 20. *See also* algae
zygotes, 13, 72, 73, 78